Cursor Movement and Deleting Shortcuts

If there's a hyphen between two keys, you must press and h... the second key. Then release both keys. If there's a comma... first key, press and release the next key, and so on.

W9-CNA-172

Press ...	To move...
↑	Up one line
Ctrl-↑	Up one paragraph
Home, ↑	To the top of the current screen
Ctrl-Home, ↑	To the top of the current page
Home, Home, ↑	To the top of a document
↓	Down one line
Ctrl-↓	Down one paragraph
Home, ↓	To the bottom of the current screen
Ctrl-Home, ↓	To the bottom of the current page
Home, Home, ↓	To the bottom of a document
→	Right a character

Press ...	To move...
Ctrl-→	To the beginning of the next word
Home, →	To the end of the screen
Home, Home, →	To the end of the line
←	Left one character
Ctrl-←	To the beginning of the previous word
Home, ←	To the beginning of the line
End	To the end of the line
Page Up	To the top of the previous page
Page Down	To the top of the next page

Deleting Text Shortcuts

Press...	To delete...
Backspace	Character to the left
Ctrl-Backspace	Current word
Home, Backspace	From cursor to the beginning of a word

Press...	To delete...
Ctrl-End	From cursor to the end of a line
Ctrl-PgDn	From cursor to the end of a page

Common Editing Tasks

If you want to...	Do this...
Highlight text	Press Alt-F4, use the cursor-movement keys to highlight the text, press Alt-F4 to turn off the highlight
Insert a code so that the date is always current	Press Shift-F5, C
Insert date text that stays the same	Press Shift-F5, T

If you want to...	Do this...
Start a new page	Press Ctrl-Enter
Check your spelling	Press Ctrl-F2, 3
Find a word	Press F2, type the word, F2
Replace all of one word/phrase with another	Press Alt-F2, N. Type the text to be replaced. Press F2. Type the replacement text. Press F2.

Common Formatting Tasks

If you want to...	Do this...
Make text bold	Press F6, type the text, press F6. Or highlight the existing text and then press F6.
Underline text	Press F8, type the text, press F8. Or highlight the existing text and then press F8.
Make text italic	Press Ctrl-F8, A, I. Type the text; then press → to turn off italic.
Indent a paragraph	Press F4 to indent on left side only. Press Shift-F4 to indent on left and right sides.
Center a line	Press Shift-F6, type the text.
Right-justify text	Press Alt-F6, type the text.
Add page numbering	Press Shift-F8, P, N, 4. Select a placement option. Press F7.

If you want to...	Do this...
Change top and bottom margins	Press Home, Home, ↑. Press Shift-F8, P, M. Type the top margin in inches and press Enter. Type the bottom margin. Press Enter, F7.
Change left and right margins	Press Shift-F8, L, M. Type the left margin in inches and press Enter. Type the right margin. Press Enter, F7.
Change line spacing	Press Shift-F8, L, S. Type the spacing you want (**1** for single spacing, **2** for double spacing, and so on). Press Enter, F7.
Center a page	Press Shift-F8, P, C, Y, F7.
Use a different font	Press Ctrl-F8, F. Highlight a font, press Enter.
Preview your document	Press Shift-F7, V. Press F7 when done.

Getting Help from WordPerfect Customer Support

If you are stuck, you can call WordPerfect Customer Support. WordPerfect customer support operators will be able to help you best if you are at your computer and in WordPerfect. They can fix the problem faster if it is a problem you can make happen more than once and explain when the problem happens. (For example, if the system freezes every time you try to print a document that has tables.)

If you're having a problem with...	Call...
Getting WordPerfect installed or running	800/533-9605
Printing on a laser printer	800/541-5170
Printing on a printer that isn't a laser printer	800/541-5160
Formatting a document	800/541-5096

If you're having a problem with...	Call...
Writing or using a macro	800/541-5129
Using graphics	800/321-3383
Anything before 7 a.m. or after 6 p.m. Mountain Time	801/222-9010 (Note that this one *isn't* a toll-free call)

I HATE WORDPERFECT®

Elden Nelson

I Hate WordPerfect

Copyright © 1993 by Que® Corporation

Library of Congress Catalog No.: 93-83381

ISBN 1-56529-212-X

95 94 93   6 5 4 3 2 1

Interpretation of the printing code: the rightmost double-digit number is the year of the book's printing; the rightmost single-digit number, the number of the book's printing. For example, a printing code of 93-1 shows that the first printing of the book occurred in 1993.

Screen reproductions in this book were created using Collage Plus from Inner Media, Inc., Hollis, NH.

I Hate WordPerfect is based on WordPerfect Version 5.1.

Publisher: Lloyd J. Short

Associate Publisher: Rick Ranucci

Publishing Plan Manager: Thomas H. Bennett

Operations Manager: Sheila Cunningham

Dedication

My friends Richard Kelly and Kelly Larsen, and my grandfather, Dr. Clyde F. Smith, were the ones who got me interested in these wacky computers in the first place. If it weren't for them, I'd probably be leading a normal, balanced, productive life. Still, I'm happy in my demented state, and thank you all for it. This book is dedicated to you, whether you like it or not.

Credits

Title Manager:
Shelley O'Hara

Production Editor:
Cindy Morrow

Technical Editor:
Gary J. Pickavet

Book Designer:
Scott Cook

Novice Reviewer:
Greg Bowers

Editorial Assistant:
Julia Blount

Production Team:

Jeff Baker
Julie Brown
Jodie Cantwell
Paula Carroll
Brad Chinn
Brook Farling
Heather Kaufman

Joy Dean Lee
Jay Lesandrini
Caroline Roop
Linda Seifert
Dennis Sheehan
Sue VandeWalle

Composed in Goudy and MCPdigital by Que Corporation.

About the Author

Elden Nelson, a Title Manager at Que Corporation, has been a documentation writer for WordPerfect Corporation where he wrote two macro manuals, as well as contributed to several other manuals. Before that, Elden worked with WordPerfect's famed Customer Support team, where he learned to sympathize with the struggles of WordPerfect users and solve their problems. Most recently, Elden has been the Senior Writer for *WordPerfect Magazine*, a monthly how-to publication for people who use WordPerfect. Elden has written dozens of articles for this magazine and continues to write a monthly column. Other jobs he's had include being an insulation salesperson, a radio disc jockey, a newspaper humor columnist, and a singer in a rock band. Go figure.

When Elden isn't agonizing over a keyboard, he can be found on a pair of rollerblades, alternately whizzing down sidewalks at tremendous speeds and bandaging himself from his most recent injury.

Finally, Elden drives—and fanatically cares for—a red Mazda Miata, is a master of the barbecue grill, is 5'8" tall, has brown hair and eyes, speaks fluent Finnish, and has never been convicted of a felony. Any questions?

Acknowledgments

Writing this book was quite a party. Thanks to everybody who made it such a fun party, especially the following people, each of which deserves a big wet kiss on the forehead (and who—I am sure—are each grateful I'll just stick to mentioning them here).

Patient and Supportive Spouse Dept.: Thanks, Susan, for doing all the cooking, cleaning, bill-paying and other yucky stuff while I tried to be single-minded about writing this book. Thanks for being an impromptu proofreader, and thanks for helping me keep what little sanity I have.

Amazingly Brilliant Staff at Que Dept.: Thanks to Shelley O'Hara, Rick Ranucci, and Don Roche for excellent coaching and guidance. Thanks also to Cindy Morrow for making sure I used verbs in most of my sentences and to Chuck Stewart for getting me involved in this project.

Cool People at *WordPerfect Magazine* Dept.: Thanks to the entire editorial staff, especially Clair Rees (who taught me the true meaning of *prolific*), Edie Rockwood (Calming Influence Extraordinaire), Allen Biehl (for so many conversations, technical and otherwise), Lisa Bearnson (or should I say "Beeernson?"), Jeff Hadfield (Kiitos kaikesta), Bryan Larsen (my birding mentor), Calvin Chipman (a great racquetball partner), Kelly Lyne (great accent, even if it doesn't sound exactly Australian), and Roger Gagon (the idea man). You're all terrific editors and good friends. Thanks also to Howard Collett—a super publisher.

Indispensable Hardware Dept.: Thanks to Dell Computers, especially Denise McLaughlin and Jill Shanks, for providing fast, trouble-free computers while I wrote this book. I guess it would have been possible for me to write this book without my Dell, but it wouldn't have been nearly as painless.

Understanding Friends and Family Dept.: Thanks to Dad, Mom, Kellene, Lori, Jodi and Christy—a great family who smiles and nods when I tell them, at great length, what I do for a living. Thanks also to Dave and Liz Payne, Bob Bringhurst, Robert Raleigh and Doug Anderson—splendid friends, one and all, who will probably find little pieces of their sense of humor in this book.

Trademark Acknowledgments

All terms mentioned in this book that are known to be trademarks or service marks have been appropriately capitalized. Que cannot attest to the accuracy of this information. Use of a term in this book should not be regarded as affecting the validity of any trademark or service mark.

DOS and Microsoft Windows are registered trademarks of Microsoft Corporation.

IBM is a registered trademark of International Business Machines, Inc.

WordPerfect is a trademark of WordPerfect Corporation.

Contents at a Glance

Table of Contents

V Impressive Stuff

15 Using Lines in Your Documents   **215**

16 Using Graphics in Your Documents   **223**

17 Using Columns   **233**

18 Using Tables   **241**

19 Speeding Things Up with Macros   **253**

Introduction

"Oh no! Not again!"

"This computer won't do what I want!"

"I hate WordPerfect!"

"Aaargh!"

Sound familiar? Welcome to the club. Computers are confusing. WordPerfect is confusing. But they don't have to be. If you hate WordPerfect, you'll love this book. This is a book about WordPerfect for people who don't want to read about WordPerfect. After all, you don't want to devote your life to your computer—you just want to type a letter.

The idea behind this book is that there's way too much in WordPerfect for any sane person to learn. This book has weeded out the bizarre, esoteric stuff and left you with the absolute essentials: bite-size chunks of WordPerfect wisdom you can use to get your work done *now*. And as an extra bonus, it's actually fun to read, so you won't instantly fall asleep every time you flip the thing open.

How This Book Is Organized

There are seven main parts to this book, which are cleverly named Part I through Part VII. These parts are divided into chapters, which are divided into sections, which are divided into paragraphs, sentences, words, letters, and, eventually, molecules. The fact is, though, that you can jump in anywhere you want. This book was written so that you don't have to read one chapter before another, or even one part of a chapter before another. If you're interested in it, read it.

If you want to get an idea of what's in each of the main sections, read on.

Part I: A Crash Course in WordPerfect

If you're brand new to WordPerfect, start in this part of the book. In fewer than 100 pages, you'll learn enough about WordPerfect that you can fake out just about any boss in America. You don't have to know a thing about WordPerfect to read these chapters.

Part II: The On-Line Editorial Assistant

Here's where you can learn to smooth out the rough spots in your work. Move text around instead of having to retype it, have the computer check your spelling, look up the right word and magically replace all of one word with a different one. This is the stuff that makes computers seem almost worth the trouble.

Part III: Formatting Essentials

Your computer isn't a typewriter—even though you may sometimes wish it were. With WordPerfect on your computer, you can do things you can only dream about with a typewriter. By knowing the tricks taught in this section, you'll be able to take care of all the day-to-day chores of deciding how the text will look on the printed page. You learn how to deal with margins, page numbering, line spacing, and all that.

Part IV: Handling Files

As you use WordPerfect, you'll need to print your text. You also will need to save your work in the computer's memory and get it back when you need it. (Sounds tougher than it is.) This part shows you how to manage those strange things called *files*, as well as how to get that work of yours onto the printed page.

Part V: Impressive Stuff

Save this part for when you're feeling a little fancy and want to show off. This part of the book covers the things in WordPerfect that most people think are "advanced," but really aren't hard at all. You'll put ruled lines, graphic pictures, newspaper columns, and table charts into your documents—no sweat.

Part VI: "I Need To Do This NOW!"

If you're under the gun and need to make a certain type of form or document, flip to this section, which gives step-by-step instructions for creating memos, letters, and form letters.

Part VII: The Quick and Dirty Dozens

If you've got two minutes, you've got enough time to learn something useful about WordPerfect. That's the idea behind The Quick and Dirty Dozens. Six lists, each containing 12 short tips about some WordPerfect topic. For instance, how about 12 Cool Things Nobody Knows You Can Do in WordPerfect, 12 Things You Should Never Do in WordPerfect, or the 12 Best WordPerfect Shortcuts? And much, much more! And all for one low price!

What about Those Drawings in the Margin?

All the information in this book is not created equal. Occasionally, the book includes something more technical than the other stuff. This book uses icons (those are the funny drawings within the margins) to say

things like, "Hey, this is technical stuff. You don't have to read it." The book has other icons that tell you when to be careful, alert you to some frustrating WordPerfect function that you'll have to deal with, and so on.

Here are the pictures and what they mean:

"I HATE THIS!"

This icon pops up whenever the book has to explain something frustrating or confusing about WordPerfect. It's a good idea to read the text next to this icon; it'll help you brace yourself for things to come.

TIP

You'll see this icon next to extra-helpful tips—things you can use to make your life easier.

CAUTION

Beware! Warning! Don't Do This! is this icon's message. It can help you avoid WordPerfect pitfalls and potholes.

EXPERTS ONLY

If you're in the mood to read more detailed information on something about WordPerfect, seek out the material flagged with this icon. This is interesting, useful stuff, but it's more advanced, and you don't have to know this information in order to use WordPerfect well.

BUZZWORDS

Computer people have made up hundreds of new words, as well as given strange new meanings to a lot of old words. This picture alerts you that one of these mysterious new terms is about to be explained.

Things Nobody Ever Reads about Books

We know that hardly anybody reads these introductions anyway, but here's some other information on how to "use" the book:

Checklist

▼ WordPerfect uses lots of things called *menus* and *messages*. These are usually questions or multiple-choice options at the bottom of the screen. To reassure you that, yes, you're in the right spot in WordPerfect, this book often has a picture of that menu or prompt. They look like this:

    Hi there! I'm a friendly menu or prompt!

▼ Sometimes you'll have to press more than one key at once. When that happens, there's a dash between the keys you're supposed to press. Press and hold down the key before the dash, and then press the key after the dash. Finally, let go of both keys.

▼ If you want to get things done in WordPerfect, you've got to press a lot of keys. When you need to press a series of keys, they'll be separated by commas and spaces. For example, if you see something that says,

Press Shift-F8, L for Line, M for Margins

you would press and hold the Shift key, press F8 (yes, there's a key on your keyboard that has an F8 on it), let go of both keys, press L, and then press M. (You can also press the lowercase versions of these letters.) Ignore the commas and spaces.

PART I

A Crash Course in WordPerfect

Includes:

CHAPTER 1

The Very Basics
(Into the Wild Blue Yonder)

IN A NUTSHELL

- ▼ Get into WordPerfect
- ▼ Know where you are
- ▼ Type text
- ▼ Move around
- ▼ Correct mistakes
- ▼ Restore deleted text
- ▼ Use the function keys

So, you hate WordPerfect. Maybe you've tried to use WordPerfect a few times and feel frustrated at your inability to make it do what you want. Or maybe you've never actually tried to use it, but just *know* you will hate it and have managed to spare yourself the agony. (I myself have never even tasted brussel sprouts for this very reason.)

In either case, you've somehow gotten yourself into a predicament: you have to use WordPerfect. What do you do now? Stop worrying. You've already made the first right move—you bought this book!

This chapter starts at the very beginning and guides you through the basics of WordPerfect. You learn how to start WordPerfect, write in WordPerfect, and then edit what you wrote. This chapter also teaches you how to get out of difficult situations.

Starting WordPerfect

(What's a nice person like you doing in a program like this?)

Starting WordPerfect isn't all that difficult. First, you turn on the computer. You see something like C:\> on-screen, followed by a blinking underline. This is called a *DOS prompt*, and it is the equivalent of computer hell.

Type **CD\WP51**, and then press Enter. If the computer spits back `Invalid Directory` or something equally incomprehensible, try typing **CD\WP**. Then press Enter.

Your screen now reads either C:\WP51 or C:\WP. To get into WordPerfect, type **WP** and press Enter.

BUZZWORDS

DOS

DOS (it rhymes with *loss*) is one of the three most-used buzzwords in the computer industry. (Never mind that I can't remember the other two right now.) DOS stands for "Disk Operating System." DOS helps your computer talk to your keyboard, disk, monitor, and programs. In other words, your computer needs DOS to run WordPerfect and other programs. When you see that cryptic `C:\>` or `C>`, you can impress onlookers by glancing haughtily at the screen and exclaiming, "Ah, I see that we're at the DOS prompt."

TIP

You can perform some wizardry to make WordPerfect start whenever you turn on the computer. If you use WordPerfect almost every time you use the computer, this can be a helpful shortcut. Snare a computer-savvy friend and try to bribe him into helping you. Here's the magic phrase you should use: "Will you please add WordPerfect to my AUTOEXEC.BAT file?" By the way, AUTOEXEC.BAT is pronounced "ought-oh-eggs-eck-dot-bat." Don't bother changing the AUTOEXEC.BAT file yourself. Because this file is vital to the proper functioning of your computer, only the technically enthusiastic should mess with it.

Checklist

▼ If this procedure doesn't work, try asking someone more technically inclined (a coworker, your wife, the paperboy) to show you how to start WordPerfect. Be sure to write down the steps so that you can start the program yourself next time.

continues

▼ When you turn on some computers, a list—rather than the DOS prompt—appears. If you turn on your computer and see a list, and if WordPerfect is on the list, you are one of the lucky few! Type the number or letter next to WordPerfect or WP on your screen. You're in!

Looking around the WordPerfect Screen

WordPerfect. Heralded as one of most powerful software tools ever created. Painstakingly detailed. Able to leap tall buildings in a single bound. So why is the screen practically blank? For the amount of money you've spent, wouldn't you expect something just a touch more exciting?

Actually, WordPerfect *is* exciting. When you get to know it, you'll be pleasantly surprised at how useful it is. Let's begin with a look at what's on-screen.

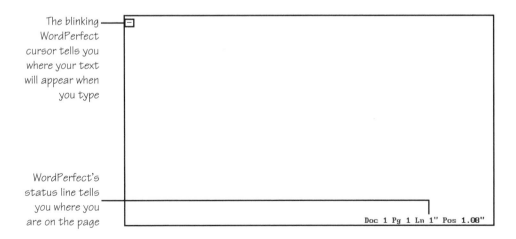

The blinking WordPerfect cursor tells you where your text will appear when you type

WordPerfect's status line tells you where you are on the page

Doc 1 Pg 1 Ln 1" Pos 1.08"

"What's That Blinking Thing?"

It's called a *cursor*. When you type words on the keyboard, they appear on-screen wherever the cursor is blinking. Think of the cursor as an on-screen "You Are Here" arrow.

Whenever you start WordPerfect, the cursor shows up in the upper left corner of the screen. The cursor moves as you type, left to right, one space at a time.

"What about Those Hieroglyphics at the Bottom of the Screen?"

The bottom of the screen looks like this:

```
Doc 1 Pg 1 Ln 1" Pos 1"
```

These letters and numbers tell you where you are (technically, where your cursor is).

Decoding the hieroglyphics

▼ *Doc* stands for "Document." *Document* is computer jargon for "Something you've typed." WordPerfect has the ability to let you work on two documents at once—sort of like having paper in two typewriters at the same time. If you see Doc 1 on-screen, you're working on the first document. If you see Doc 2, you're working on the second.

▼ *Pg* is not the rating of your document. Pg will not change to G when you write Disney stories, and it will not change to R when you write a steamy novel. Pg does stand for "Page." If you see Pg 1,

continues

you're on the first page. **Pg 2** means you're on the second page. **Pg 972** means you're on page 972 and should consider being a tad more concise.

▼ *Ln* means "Line." This number tells you how many inches you are from the top of the page. Because WordPerfect automatically sets up 1-inch margins all the way around your document, this area shows 1" when you are at the top of a page. (**Note:** You do not actually see the 1-inch margin on-screen, but when you print a document, it will have a 1-inch margin.)

▼ *Pos* means "Position." This number tells you how many inches you are from the left side of the page. Again, because WordPerfect automatically sets up margins of 1 inch all the way around your document, this area shows 1" when you are the left edge of the page. Because this number changes with every single letter you type, it's an excellent thing to ignore.

EXPERTS ONLY

Pos can tell you a lot more about what's going on in WordPerfect than you want to know

▼ If Pos changes to POS, your Caps Lock key is turned on. Any text you type will appear in capital letters. Press the key again to turn off Caps Lock. POS changes back to Pos when you turn off Caps Lock.

▼ If Pos is flashing, your Num Lock key is on. Press the Num Lock key to turn it off.

▼ The number to the right of Pos tells you whether you have selected bold, underline, italic, or other special features. On some computers, the appearance of the number will reflect

EXPERTS ONLY

the selected feature: 1" becomes 1' when the italic feature is selected. On most computers, the 1" appears with some arbitrarily selected color background, and you are supposed to remember which color background represents each feature.

Typing Text

(Writing the Great American Novel)

Typing in WordPerfect is a lot like using your typewriter, but easier in lots of ways. First, you don't press Enter at the end of each line. WordPerfect automatically "wraps" the text to the next line. To see how WordPerfect knows when to go to the next line, type frantically at the keyboard for a minute. Try typing the following text without pressing Enter:

> Judy, listening intently to the company president give the yearly review, realized she preferred Cocoa Puffs to Count Chocula.

As you type, the cursor moves to the right, outrunning the letters. As you get to the end of a line, WordPerfect knows the line should end and zips down to the beginning of the next line. WordPerfect automatically creates soft line breaks (*soft returns*). Later, when you add text or make changes to the text, WordPerfect adjusts the line breaks.

You add text just by typing it in. As you type the text, everything following the cursor (the text you typed previously) is pushed down to clear space for the new text. This is perhaps the second most wonderful thing about using a word processor—and it's environmentally correct! Think of all the paper (and therefore trees) it saves; no more crumpled paper filling the garbage can!

BUZZWORDS

HARD LINE BREAKS

Hard line breaks (also called *hard returns*) are inserted when you press Enter. These breaks will not be adjusted when you insert or delete text. Soft line breaks (also called *soft returns*) are inserted by WordPerfect and do adjust as you insert or delete text.

The Multipurpose Enter Key

Don't completely forget about the Enter key. You still need it in certain situations—for example, to separate paragraphs. Simply press the Enter key when you want a paragraph to end.

You also use it to add blank lines between lines of text. And to end lines before they wrap to the next line. For example, a name or address usually doesn't go from margin to margin. Instead, type your name and press Enter. The cursor moves to the beginning of the next line, where you can type your address.

Other keys you need to know about when typing

▼ Press Tab when you want the first line of a paragraph indented. In fact, the Tab key works the same in WordPerfect as it does on a typewriter.

▼ The Caps Lock key works the same as it does on a typewriter (makes letters capitals)...almost. For some reason, it only works on letters, not on the number keys.

Breaking Pages

After you type for a while, you fill up the screen (unless you are typing something remarkably short, like the New Year's resolutions you stuck to). At that point, the text you wrote earlier moves off the top of the screen, making room for new words at the bottom of the screen. DO NOT PANIC. The top line of your text *hasn't* fallen off the face of the earth; it's just moved off the top of your screen. You simply can't see it.

If you type long enough, you'll fill up a page. WordPerfect can tell when the page you're working on doesn't have any more space, and it then gives you a new page. It separates the pages for you on-screen with a dashed line, which looks like this:

- -

Everything above the dashed line is on one page; everything below the dashed line is on the next page. As you fill up each page, a new row of dashed lines appears, signaling that you have begun a new page.

Sometimes you'll want to end a page before it's full of text, like after you've created a title page or when you want to end a book chapter. You can repeatedly press the Enter key until a page break appears, but this method is cumbersome and unnecessary.

A better method is to hold down the Ctrl key and press Enter. A page break appears at the position of the cursor. Look closely. This page break is not the same single-dashed line that separates your other pages. It's a double-dashed line:

===

BUZZWORDS

HARD AND SOFT PAGE BREAKS

The double-dashed line is called a *hard page break*, and the single-dashed line is called a *soft page break*. The locations of soft page breaks change as you add and delete text so that the page contains the same number of lines. Hard page breaks, on the other hand, do not change when text is added or deleted; the page always ends at the position of the page break, no matter how few lines of text are on the page.

Moving Around

(Let your fingers do the typing)

You move the cursor by using the arrow keys. Look on your keyboard for a cluster of arrow keys pointing in different directions (up, down, left, and right). These keys show up in different places on different keyboards, in accordance with the computer manufacturer mandate that no two keyboards look or work exactly the same. On most keyboards, though, the arrow keys are in their own lonely little cluster just right of the letter keys.

Basically, the cursor moves in the direction indicated by the arrow. Press the down-arrow key. The cursor moves down one line of text (although not past the last word in the document). Press the right-arrow key. The cursor moves one letter to the right. You just press the arrow keys until the cursor is positioned where you need to edit text.

Amazing but true facts about moving your cursor

▼ You can't move the cursor past the end of the last word in the document. The cursor only goes as far as you've typed.

▼ If you hold down a cursor key, it goes completely berserk. For example, if you hold down the up-arrow key, the cursor begins rocketing toward the top of the document. The cursor continues its mad ascent until you release the up-arrow key.

▼ If you press the left-arrow key when you're already at the left edge of the page, the cursor moves to the right edge of the page, one line up.

▼ If you have more than a screenful of text and you press the right-arrow key when the cursor is at the right edge of a line, the cursor goes to the left side of the page, one line down.

▼ If the cursor is at the top of the screen and you press the up-arrow key, the text moves (computer types call this *scrolling*) down so that you can see text above it.

▼ Pressing the down-arrow key when you're at the bottom of the document produces the opposite effect: the old text moves up so that you can see the text below it.

Speed Movement Keys

When you start writing your Great American Novel (or at least creating long documents), you'll find that using the arrow keys to move your cursor through large sections of text is too slo-o-o-ow. WordPerfect has

several difficult-to-remember keystroke combinations that quickly get you from one place to another. Even though these keystrokes initially seem complicated, after some practice, your fingers will remember them.

Key or key combo	What the key or combo does
Home, Home, ↑	Moves the cursor to the top of your document. You press the Home key twice, and then press the up-arrow key.
Home, Home, ↓	Moves the cursor to the end of your document.
Ctrl-→	Moves the cursor to the beginning of the next word.
Ctrl-←	Moves the cursor to the beginning of the previous word. In case you were wondering, there are no key combinations to move to the *end* of the next or previous word.
Ctrl-↑	Moves the cursor to the beginning of the previous paragraph.
Ctrl-↓	Moves the cursor to the beginning of the next paragraph.
Page Up	Moves the cursor to the beginning of the previous page. This key is sometimes labeled PgUp—kind of like reading shorthand.
Page Down	Moves the cursor to the beginning of the next page. This key is sometimes labeled PgDn.

Correcting Small Mistakes

(Throw your white-out in the trash)

I'm a lousy typist. I tend to hit the "C" when I meant to type "V" and it's pretty much a coin toss as to whether I land on the right key when I aim for the "M."

It's okay to be a miserable typist in WordPerfect, though. Cleaning up typos is *no sweat*. Removing an unwanted word is just as easy. You just need to become handy with the Backspace and Delete keys.

Pressing the Backspace key removes the character to the left of the cursor. The Backspace key is located in the upper right corner of the letters part of your keyboard. Some Backspace keys are kind enough to be labeled with the word *Backspace*, while others have nothing but an arrow pointing left. Do not confuse this key with the left arrow key, which does not delete text.

Pressing Delete removes the character that's over the top of your cursor. (Use this key to delete text to the right of your cursor.) Look for a key labeled "Del" or "Delete."

CAUTION

If you hold down the Backspace or Delete key rather than pressing it just once or twice, WordPerfect starts erasing at a furious rate. You often end up deleting a lot more than you wanted to. Don't hold down these keys unless you've got tons of text to erase.

Bringing Text Back from the Dead

When you're new to WordPerfect, you're bound to make a lot of little mistakes. As you get more practice, you'll find that your mistakes become much bigger. Just kidding. One mistake you might make—frequently—is deleting text that you really wanted to keep.

When you delete text, it isn't really gone—at least, not right away. You can use the F1 key to "cancel" your most recent deletion.

BUZZWORDS

FUNCTION KEYS

Function keys are labeled F1 to F10 or F1 to F12 and appear along the left or top of your keyboard. These keys are used to access features of a program. Every program uses the function keys in a different way.

Try experimenting with "undeleting" text. Type **The most important thing in the world**. Now press Backspace enough times to delete the entire sentence. You've just deleted The Most Important Thing in the World! Well, not to worry, you can bring it back. Press F1. A message appears at the bottom of the screen. Press 1. The most important thing in the world is back!

CAUTION

Don't delay bringing back text that's been deleted. Do it as soon as possible. WordPerfect can only hold three deleted pieces of text, and it's easy to lose the one you want if you're not careful.

Those $#&! Function Keys

In WordPerfect, you press a function key or a function key combination to access a particular feature. For instance, to undelete text, you press F1.

WordPerfect gives each key a "name." The F1 key is affectionately known as the Cancel key. The F7 key is the Exit key. WordPerfect prima donnas like to throw these names around to show off. You don't need to worry about the name.

You also shouldn't worry about memorizing the function of each key. First, there's nothing intuitive about which key does what. Why F1 for Cancel and F2 for Search? Why not? Second, there are at least 30 combinations of function keys. (You can press just the function key, Shift and the function key, Alt and the function key, and Ctrl and the function key.) You will use only a few function keys. And after you use WordPerfect for a while, you'll get used to the most common keys.

TIP

When you want to use a function key combination (such as Alt-F2), press and hold down the first key (Alt). Then press the second key (F2). Release both keys.

EXPERTS ONLY

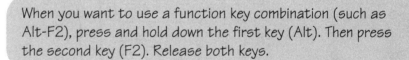

We're not in Kansas anymore!

So far you've been spared the tangle of screens, prompts, and menus that makes up most of WordPerfect's features. Eventually, however, you'll feel brave and fearless and wander off into what is known as the "WordPerfect maze." One menu will lead to another to another until you're miles from home. And leaving bread crumbs won't help find your way back. (Trust me; I've tried.) To get back to the WordPerfect you know, press F1 until you return to the document screen.

CHAPTER 2

Editing Text
(Rewriting History)

IN A NUTSHELL

▼ Delete text
▼ Undelete text

Wordperfect is an editor's dream. With it, you can slash words, lines, or even pages with the greatest of ease. And if you change your mind, you can reverse the situation faster than you can say "Oops!" This chapter shows you how to erase any amount of text at one time—from a single word to whole pages.

Deleting Text

(Using that big WordPerfect eraser)

If you don't like the text you've written, delete it. The Delete and Backspace keys are great for deleting a few letters at a time, but they really get annoying when you want to erase a long word or a whole line. You have to either hold down the key and hope you can let go before WordPerfect erases more than you want, or tap the key over and over and over until you've gotten rid of the words you don't need.

You've got some much faster—and more precise—tools at your disposal for erasing more than just a couple of letters.

Delete a Word

When you want to delete a single word, move the cursor so that it's anywhere in that word; then press Ctrl-Backspace. The word and the space after the word are gone.

EXPERTS ONLY

Fine-tooth distinctions you can skip

If you are boning up on WordPerfect key-combination trivia, here are some additional alternatives:

▼ You can press Ctrl-Delete instead of Ctrl-Backspace. They both do the same thing.

▼ If the cursor is between two words when you press Ctrl-Backspace, the word to the *left* of the cursor is deleted.

▼ If the cursor is in the middle of a word and you want to delete to the beginning of the word, press Home, Backspace.

▼ Press Home, Delete to delete from the cursor to the beginning of the next word.

Erase from the Cursor to the End of the Line

Sometimes you'll get really aggressive with your editing, and you'll want to get rid of whole strings of words. To delete from your cursor to the end of the line, just press Ctrl-End. Everything from the cursor to the end of the line disappears. If there's any text on the following line, it moves up to take the place of the deleted text.

TIP

Ctrl-End doesn't delete the whole line; it only deletes from the cursor to the end of the line. If you want to delete an *entire* line, press Home, Home, left-arrow key to move the cursor to the beginning of the line. Then press Ctrl-End.

Delete from the Cursor to the End of the Page

If you're disgusted with the latter half of a page of text, move the cursor to where you want the deletion to begin; then press Ctrl-Page Down. WordPerfect asks

```
Delete Remainder of page? No (Yes)
```

Press Y. Presto! You have erased everything from the cursor to the end of the page.

TIP

> Pressing Ctrl-Page Down doesn't delete everything on the page—just everything from your cursor to the end of the page. If you want to delete *everything* on the page, move the cursor to the beginning of that page by pressing Page Up, then Page Down. Now press Ctrl-Page Down. Everything on the page is erased.

Erase Any Amount of Text

Deleting words, lines, and pages is all well and good, but sometimes what you want to get rid of doesn't fall neatly into one of these categories—you just want to erase a specific amount of text. You can delete a chunk of text—anything from a paragraph to several pages—most efficiently by using the Block feature.

The idea behind Block is that you mark a certain amount of text, just as if you were highlighting it with one of those fluorescent pink pens. This is how you mark the text you want to erase:

1. Move the cursor to the beginning of the text to erase.

Your cursor should be right under the first character that you want to take out of the document.

2. Press Alt-F4.

`Block On` appears in the lower left corner of the screen. That's WordPerfect's way of telling you it's ready for you to mark the text.

3. Use the arrow keys to move to the end of the text you want to erase.

As you move the cursor, you see that everything from your beginning point to your cursor is highlighted. When you finish, your cursor should be right after the last character you want to delete.

4. Press Backspace or Delete.

When you press one of these keys, WordPerfect asks you

        `Delete Block? No (Yes)`

5. Press Y for Yes.

The marked text disappears.

Checklist

▼ If you start blocking text to delete and change your mind, press F1 to turn off Block. You can also press Alt-F4 or F12 to turn off Block.

▼ You don't have to start blocking at the beginning of the text to delete; if you want, you can start at the end and block to the beginning. WordPerfect is flexible. This flexibility is useful if your cursor is closer to the end of the text you want to delete than the beginning.

continues

▼ When the `Block On` prompt is on, you can't type text. If you decide you need to type something before you delete the chunk of text, press F1 to turn off Block, type what you need, and then mark the text to be deleted.

▼ There are only a few times a mouse is useful in WordPerfect—blocking text is one of them. If you have a mouse, use it to move the mouse pointer (a little rectangle that moves on-screen when you move the mouse on your desk) to the place you want to begin deleting. Press and hold down the left mouse button, and then slide the mouse to position the mouse pointer where you want to end deleting. Let go of the mouse button and press Delete, Y.

▼ There's a lot more to learn about Block. In fact, Chapter 7 talks of nothing else.

Restoring Deleted Text for Fun and Profit

Any time you erase something, WordPerfect remembers it. In fact, WordPerfect remembers the *three* most recent things you've deleted—and you can get them back if you need them.

To get back the text you've deleted most recently, press F1, P. You can also get back the two deletions before that, as well. So if you block and delete a paragraph, then move down a couple of lines and delete a word, then move down to the bottom of the document and erase the whole last page, you haven't really lost anything. You can get back any of those three most recent deletions.

This is how you get back your second-most-recent or third-most-recent deletion:

1. Move the cursor to where the deleted text ought to go.

When you restore the text, WordPerfect plops it right at the position of the cursor.

2. Press F1, then P for Previous.

Your second-most-recent deletion appears highlighted at the cursor position. If you want to see the third-most-recent deletion, press P for Previous again. Make sure that the highlighted text is really the text that you want back.

3. Press R for Restore.

The highlighted text gets put back into your document.

Checklist

▼ If you don't want to insert the deleted text, press F1 to cancel.

▼ You only get to restore your three most recent deletions; anything later than that is gone. So, it's important to restore text as soon as possible.

▼ What counts as a "deletion?" All of the text you delete until you do something else. If you delete an entire page before you move the cursor or stop typing, that whole page counts as a deletion. If you just erase one letter before you type or move, that single letter counts as a deletion.

continues

▼ Deleting and restoring is a great way to move text from one point in your document to another. Just delete the text you want to move; then, before you do anything else, move the cursor to the new position for the text. Press F1, R to place the text.

▼ If you press P for Previous again, WordPerfect doesn't show you the fourth-most-recent deletion. Instead, it cycles back to the most recent deletion.

TIP

Oh, eye'm shure the spelling's all rite

Just typing and editing your document isn't enough—you also need to check the spelling. Chapter 8 has the lowdown on using WordPerfect's Speller.

CHAPTER 3

Save Your Work

(Save Your Sanity)

IN A NUTSHELL

- ▼ Name your document
- ▼ Update your document
- ▼ Turn on the Automatic Backup feature
- ▼ Recover your document
- ▼ Clear the document screen
- ▼ Quit WordPerfect

After you create a work of genius, you need to save it. First, you name *and* save the document. Then you just save (update) it. This chapter covers both tasks. You also learn how to clear the document screen *without* saving what you've written. After all, you'll write some things that you just won't want to keep—such as that sonnet about dental floss. Finally, you learn how to get out of WordPerfect.

What "Save" Means

(Rescue 911)

If anything can make you hate WordPerfect (as well as computers in general), losing your hard work is it. Imagine that you've been working on a report. You're typing along faster than you ever have before—after all, you need to be finished in 57 minutes. Suddenly lightning strikes and knocks out the power in your home. What happens to all your work?

The fact is, every time the computer is turned off—whether on purpose or by accident—it forgets everything. If there's a power failure or if your computer unexpectedly "locks up" (refuses to budge because of some problem with the program), you could very well lose all your typing. To avoid this problem, you need to "save" your document.

Save means to take the document you've been typing and store a copy of it on your hard disk. (You never see your hard disk because it's permanently bolted into the insides of your computer—just think of it as a big filing cabinet inside your computer.)

After a document is saved, you can retrieve your work and come back to it another time.

DOCUMENT

Unless you are in the legal field, you probably aren't used to referring to pieces of writing as *documents*. You probably wouldn't say "Jane, get me the Company Picnic Document." In computerese, a *document* is a collection of writing—a poem, memo, letter, report. A document can be of any length—one line, a couple paragraphs, several pages.

Saving Your Document

To ensure that you never have to go through the agony of losing your work and having to retype it, get into the habit of saving your documents after every few paragraphs that you type. This is how you save a document:

1. Press F10.

   As soon as you do this, a question appears at the bottom of the screen:

   `Document to be saved:`

   Whenever you save a document, you give it a name so that you can find it again.

FILE NAME

When you save a document—any kind of document—you give it a name. That name is called the *file name*. For the most part, *file* and *document* mean the same thing.

2. Type a file name, such as **MYFIRST.DOC**.

You have to follow some strict rules when naming files. You can use only 11 characters: an 8-character "first" name and a 3-character "last" name. A period separates the two names. You can't use spaces and you shouldn't use punctuation. That leaves you with letters and numbers. Take a look at "The Name Game" section for the small print on these rules and regulations.

3. Press Enter.

After you've saved your document, the name you gave it (as well as some information about where it's kept) appears in the lower left corner of your screen, like this:

```
C:\WP51\DOCS\MYFIRST.DOC
```

Checklist

▼ You can *change* the name of a document by using the steps for naming a document. When WordPerfect asks you for the name of the document (step 2 in the preceding steps), type the new name. The new name replaces the old name.

▼ It's important to make your document names memorable. After a while, you'll have a lot of documents—each with a different name—and it's easy to confuse and forget names. You might want to name a document FRED if you're writing a letter to Fred.

▼ You can type the name in uppercase or lowercase. When the file name is displayed on-screen and in file lists, it will appear in all uppercase no matter how you type it.

▼ You might type a name that's already been used. If you do, a message appears: `Replace Filename? No (Yes)`. This means you already have a file by the name you just typed. If you want to replace the file on-screen with the file you've saved previously, press Y. If you don't or you are not sure, press N for No; then type in a different name.

Knowing Where Your Files are Kept (The path less traveled by)

`C:\WP51\DOCS` is called the *path*. The path is like a road map pointing to where your file is kept. You can use your Little Orphan Annie secret decoder pin and the following to decipher the message:

▼ `C:` means the file is on your C drive, which is your hard disk. (If this reads `A:` or `B:`, the file is on one of your floppy disks.)

▼ `\WP51` is the first *directory*. A directory is similar to a folder in your filing cabinet. You store related documents in one folder. Paths and directories are all part of that cryptic DOS program that everyone loves to hate. More about directories later.

▼ `\DOCS` means that there's another directory inside your \WP51 directory.

The path gives DOS directions so that DOS can find the file. The path essentially says: Start at the C: drive, look in the WP51 directory, and then go to the DOCS directory; there you'll find the file.

The Name Game

DOS imposes some strict rules when it comes to file names. DOS is big on rules. If you don't follow these rules when you name your documents, you'll see an error message or WordPerfect will make up its own name (basically chopping off what won't fit).

Rules to keep in mind when naming documents

▼ The name can consist of two parts. A "first" name and a "last" name. You use a period to separate the two. For example, in the file name BANANA.SPL, BANANA is the first name, SPL is the last name, and the period separates the two names.

▼ The first name can have up to eight characters—but doesn't have to use all eight. The last name can have up to three characters, but it doesn't have to use all three. HOTFUDG.SUN is acceptable, CARAMELFUDGE.SUN is not (the first name is too long).

▼ The file must have the first name, but you don't have to add a last name. PARFAIT is OK.

▼ Don't use spaces. DILLY BAR won't work. WordPerfect will use only the characters before the space. So if you try this file name, WordPerfect will save the document as DILLY.

▼ Stick to using letters and numbers in your file names. Except for that period between the first and last name, avoid punctuation. #$!%CHUB won't work.

TIP

Use the file's last name, called the *extension*, to show how files are related. For instance, all LTR files might belong to the LETTER clan. All MMO files might be MEMOS.

CHAPTER 3

Updating Your Document

(Save early, save often)

Save your work regularly—every three paragraphs or so. The document on-screen will change as you continue to work on it, but the document on disk reflects only the work you did up to the point you last saved. You still have the potential to lose work unless you save often.

Here's how you update a document:

1. Press F10.

A message appears, `Document to be saved:`, along with the name that you gave to the file earlier. You don't need to type the file name again—WordPerfect remembers it.

2. Press Enter.

You're asked whether you want to *replace* the document, which sounds a little intimidating. The prompt would be better if it asked whether you want to *update* the document, because that's what you are doing: updating (replacing) the document on the disk with your latest, greatest changes and additions.

3. Press Y for Yes.

TIP

When you're updating your documents, WordPerfect's prompts are much more of a nuisance than an assistance. The best way to update your documents is to just press F10, Enter, Y. Get used to those keystrokes and just use them. Don't even bother looking at the prompts when you're updating documents.

TIP

Besides updating your documents every few minutes, make sure that you save whenever you make a difficult or elaborate change that you just don't want to duplicate. For example, whenever I spend a long time struggling with how to explain a difficult idea and I finally get the wording right, I save right away.

Setting Up Automatic Backup

(Better safe than sorry)

WordPerfect has a feature that was designed to make those inevitable disasters—blackouts, computer crashes, and clumsy electricians—a little more bearable. This feature is called Automatic Backup. You tell WordPerfect to make a spare copy (*backup*) of your work every so often. If something ugly happens, you can use the backup.

You have to set WordPerfect to do automatic backups only once, so don't try to memorize the steps or worry about the menu options that pop up. Just follow these steps: Press Shift-F1. Press E to select Environment, B to select Backup Options, T to select Timed Document Backup, and then Y. You see a screen that looks like this:

```
Setup: Backup

      Timed backup files are deleted when you exit WP normally.  If you
      have a power or machine failure, you will find the backup file in the
      backup directory indicated in Setup: Location of Files.

         Backup Directory                      C:\WP51

      1 - Timed Document Backup                Yes (No)
          Minutes Between Backups              30


      Original backup will save the original document with a .BK! extension
      whenever you replace it during a Save or Exit.

      2 - Original Document Backup             No




   Selection: 1
```

Here's where you tell WordPerfect to make automatic backups of your work.

If your screen looks different, you probably took a wrong turn somewhere. Press F1 until you're back at the document screen; then try again.

To decide how often, ask yourself this question: What's the greatest amount of work I could bear to lose? Half an hour? Fifteen minutes? Type the number of minutes; then press Enter, and then F7. WordPerfect will now make a spare copy of your document as often as you specified.

TIP

Do not think that this Automatic Backup system means you don't have to save your documents. Automatic Backup only makes copies periodically. If Murphy's Law goes into effect and your power goes off between backups, the backup won't include your most recent work. This work will reflect only the changes made up to the last backup. Bottom line: Still save your document!

Disaster Strikes

"It" happens to everyone. You are cheerfully typing along when the un-thinkable happens. The power goes out or the computer locks up. Uh-oh. I just hope you've been following the advice in this chapter!

Yes! I *Did* Set the Automatic Backup

If you set the Automatic Backup, you should be able to get most of your work back. First, start WordPerfect the way you usually do. Instead of jumping into the familiar editing screen, WordPerfect stays at the startup screen, and this message appears at the bottom of the screen:

```
Are other copies of WordPerfect currently running? (Y/N)
```

Press N for No. When you do this, a new message appears:

```
Old document 1 backup file exists. 1 Rename; 2 Delete: 1
```

The "backup file" is the spare copy WordPerfect made for you. Press 1. You see yet another prompt:

```
New Name:
```

Type a file name, and then press Enter. In the lower left corner of the screen, the path and file name appear, something like this:

```
C:\WP51\BACKUP
```

Write down this name (path and file) exactly as you see it. Then press Enter to go into the WordPerfect screen. Here, press Shift-F10, type

what you just wrote on the paper, and press Enter. You see WordPerfect's backup copy of your document. Chances are, it won't have all your most recent changes, but it *will* have those up to the point the last backup was made. If the backup document is acceptable, save the document with a new name—one that has more to do with what the document actually contains. Or, if you were working on a document that was already named, use that name.

If you have a more recent copy of the document than the backup, clear the screen and open the latest copy. "Opening" documents is explained in the next chapter.

Oh No! I *Didn't* Set the Automatic Backup!

If you didn't set the Automatic Backup feature, you can get instead the last version you saved. Chapter 4 fills you in on how to retrieve a document. And if you didn't save the document, go directly to the start of this chapter; do not pass Go, do not collect $200.

Exiting Documents and WordPerfect

(Playing 20 questions)

You can type for only so long. Then your eyes stop focusing, you use adjectives where you should use adverbs, and your sentences read, "See Spot. See Spot run. See Spot run some more." It's definitely time to work on something else, or better yet, to take a break and go catch up with the Flintstones.

Before you can leave your document or turn off your computer, you need to exit WordPerfect. Remember how you had to master the art of getting

into WordPerfect? Well, there's an art to getting out, too. WordPerfect likes to play a game of 20 questions when you want to leave a document or WordPerfect.

Here's the first question: Do you want to totally escape (exit WordPerfect), or do you just want to start again with a new sheet of "paper" (a clean, new document)?

I Want Out!

OK. You want out. But you don't get off that easily. You have to decide what to do with the stuff you've typed on-screen. You have several choices at this point:

▼ **You *don't* want to save the document**
To quit WordPerfect without saving your work, press F7. Then press N when asked `Save Document?` Finally, press Y at the `Exit WP?` question. You're free, free at last!

▼ **You *do* want to save the document**
If you haven't saved your document by the time you're ready to leave WordPerfect, you are in big trouble with the Save Police. And you're lucky you have something to save. Press F7, Y when asked `Save Document?` Then type a file name for your document. Press Enter, and then Y when asked `Exit WP?`

▼ **You've already saved the document**
You've been working along, saving your document every few minutes, just like you ought to, and now you're ready to go home. Here's how to save your latest changes and get out of the program: Press F7, Y at the `Save Document?` question; then press Enter to update your changes; finally, press Y at the `Exit WP?` question.

I Want a Clean Sheet of "Paper"

Say that you're not quite ready to quit. You just want a new document on-screen. WordPerfect first makes you contend with the current on-screen document. Here are your choices:

Checklist

▼ **You *don't* want to save the document**
If you write a few sentences and want to give up and start over (rumple up that piece of paper and get a new one), you can clear the document window and start from a new, clean screen. Press F7, press N at the `Save Document?` question, and then press N at the `Exit WP?` question.

▼ **You *do* want to save the document**
If you've been working on a document, haven't saved it yet, and want to start working on something different, you've come to the right place. Press F7, press Y at the `Save Document?` question, and then type a file name for your document. Press Enter, and then press N at the `Exit WP?` question.

▼ **You've already saved the document**
No more writer's block. You're finished with one document, you're on a roll, and you're ready for the next document. Press F7, press Y at the `Save Document?` question, press Enter to update your changes, and then press N at the `Exit WP?` question.

Oops! I Changed My Mind

Any time during the exit 20 questions process, you can tell WordPerfect that you've changed your mind and *don't* want to leave after all—just press F1. The questions disappear, the interrogation ends, and you can get back to work.

CAUTION

Don't just turn off the computer when you're done typing for the day. You can damage program files if you don't make a graceful exit. Make sure that you *always* completely exit WordPerfect first.

I Can't Possibly Remember All This Stuff!

Use these two charts to help speed along the decision-making. If you want, you can photocopy the charts and tape them to the bottom of your keyboard.

I Want a Clean Sheet of Paper

	DO save the document	DON'T save the document
Document already has a name	F7, Y, Enter, Y, N	F7, N, N
Document doesn't have a name	F7, Y, type a new file name, Enter, N	F7, N, N

I Want Out!

	DO save the document	DON'T save the document
Document already has a name	F7, Y, Enter, Y, Y	F7, N, Y
Document doesn't have a name	F7, Y, type a new file name, Enter, Y	F7, N, Y

CHAPTER 4

Retrieving Your Documents

IN A NUTSHELL

▼ See a list of files you've created

▼ Display a document on-screen (retrieve it)

▼ Preview a document before you retrieve it

▼ Retrieve a document really quickly

When you name and save a document, the computer stores that document in a file on your hard disk. (Most people refer to a *document* as the text on-screen and to a *file* as the text stored on disk. But the terms really refer to the same thing.)

Once the document is on disk, you can "retrieve" it—display it again on-screen so that you can make changes. This chapter teaches you how. (You'll also have to understand a little bit about how documents are stored—directories and paths and such.)

Displaying Your Documents

Chapter 3 explains how to name and save your documents so that you can work on them again later. To help you find the document you want, you can display a list of documents, and then choose one from that list. Here is how you display the list:

1. Press F5.

A message appears at the bottom of the screen, like this:

```
Dir C:\WP51\DOCS\*.*
```

This message tells you what set of files you will be looking at. Here, you will be seeing all files that are in the WP51\DOCS directory.

2. Press Enter.

A new screen appears. There's a lot of stuff, but you can ignore most of it. The important thing about this screen is that it shows two columns of names (the documents you saved) and numbers, divided by a line.

The directory currently being shown

File names are sorted alphabetically

Use arrow keys to move the highlight bar

```
01-22-93  08:47p              Directory C:\WP51\DATA\*.*
Document size:        910  Free:169,488,384 Used:   1,773,711       Files:        112

.     Current   <Dir>                      ..   Parent    <Dir>
JOURNAL .         <Dir>  01-22-93 08:47p   LETTERS .         <Dir>  01-22-93 08:47p
NOVEL   .         <Dir>  01-22-93 08:47p   1JANET  .        19,469  12-12-92 05:41p
1JANET  .SCN    13,366  01-18-93 09:08p    2JANET  .SCN    14,326  01-20-93 10:46a
340R    .SUS    33,439  06-26-91 09:19a    APES    .       27,722  05-24-92 01:55p
BACK    .        9,875  09-07-91 03:33p    BATH    .1      28,533  04-25-92 10:56a
BBS     .DOC    22,483  11-25-90 09:42p    BIBLIO  .        5,445  05-02-92 05:13p
BIBLIO  .SUS     3,461  03-13-90 08:30p    BIBLIO2 .        6,298  12-17-91 11:01p
BINDING .DOC    24,979  10-21-90 07:59p    BUCKS   .        7,423  12-05-91 01:18p
CAESAR  .       16,062  05-27-91 05:35p    CAL     .FRM    37,318  11-10-91 12:42p
CASECALL.DOC    18,813  02-13-90 12:10a    CIVILWAR.        7,457  06-04-91 01:17p
CODE    .DOC    11,737  03-25-92 07:56p    CODE    .SCN    12,022  03-25-92 07:51p
COM     .       17,963  12-18-91 10:15p    COM     .WCM     3,393  06-06-92 07:55p
COMIC   .       15,455  08-10-90 12:26a    COMMANDS.DOC    16,529  04-14-90 06:14p
COVER   .       17,106  10-28-92 09:23p    DOSGYGE .        6,733  02-26-91 10:48p
DOSUSWIN.DOC    27,971  07-01-91 07:08a    DOZEN   .       36,535  12-26-92 05:32p
DRAGNET .        9,557  03-05-91 09:43p    DRAGNET2.DOC     6,820  03-12-91 08:37p
DUCK    .       15,955  07-13-90 09:36a    DUMMIES .NTS    31,822  12-08-92 11:36p
DUMMIES .RPT    78,042  12-08-92 11:51p ▼  EQLESSON.210     5,623  02-10-90 09:45p

1 Retrieve; 2 Delete; 3 Move/Rename; 4 Print; 5 Short/Long Display;
6 Look; 7 Other Directory; 8 Copy; 9 Find; N Name Search: 6
```

Beside each file name is a number telling you how big the file is.

Checklist

▼ On the left side of each column are the names of the files themselves. WordPerfect automatically alphabetizes these files. The first
file is in the top left corner, the second is in the top right, then left,
then right, and on and on. The alphabetization goes from left to
right, top to bottom.

▼ Beside each file name is a number telling you how big the file is.
Ignore this number.

▼ On the right side of each column is the date and time the files were
last worked on. This information can be helpful if you've got two
versions of the same document and want to figure out which is
the most current. Usually, however, you can just ignore this
information.

▼ A bar highlights one file at a time. Use this bar to highlight the file
you want to retrieve.

continues

Checklist Continued

▼ You can move around in List Files in the same way you would move in a document. Press the down-arrow key; the bar moves down. Press the up-arrow key; the bar moves up.

▼ After you've highlighted a file, you can either look at it to see if it's the one you want (see "Using the Look Option"), or you can take a leap of faith and just retrieve the file (see "Retrieving Documents in WordPerfect").

▼ After you've used WordPerfect for a while, you'll have more files than can fit on one screen. When that happens, use the arrow keys to scroll up and down in the list. Use the Page Up and Page Down keys to move up or down a whole screenful of files.

TIP

List Files can help you avoid some DOS tasks. You can move, copy, print, delete, and much, much more from this screen. In fact, just about everything you've ever had to do at DOS, you can do more easily in List Files. If you're interested, Chapter 14 is completely dedicated to this magnificent feature.

Retrieving Documents in WordPerfect

(Fetch, Fido)

In WordPerfect lingo, *retrieving* means to bring up a document you've worked on previously. You *retrieve* a document when you want to work on it again. Start from a blank document screen. If you just started WordPerfect, you should see the blank document screen. If you've typed something, you need to clear the document (see Chapter 3).

Next, press F5, Enter to go to List Files. Then highlight the file you want and press R for Retrieve. The document that you highlighted appears on-screen.

"I HATE THIS!"

Hey! The document's on-screen, but I can't edit it!

You might be tempted to press Enter instead of R to retrieve the document (which would the simple way). If you do, the screen will *look* like you've retrieved the document, but you'll soon find you're living in a fool's paradise: you can't edit the document because you've chosen Look instead of Retrieve. To escape, just press F1 to go back to the list of files.

Checklist

▼ If you're in List Files and decide you don't want to retrieve a file after all, press F1 to go back to the document screen.

▼ When you press R to retrieve the document, you may get a message reading `Retrieve into current document? No (Yes)`. This means that you already have a document on-screen. Press N for No, and then press F1 to go back to the document screen. Clear the document screen; then go back to List Files and try again.

▼ After you've retrieved the document, you can get to work editing it. Remember, though, that you have to save your changes.

EXPERTS ONLY

Confessions of a directory user

WordPerfect automatically goes to a certain directory each time you press F5, Enter. If you want to go to a different directory, press F5, and then type a different directory name, such as **C:\WP51\DOCS\LETTERS**. (The "full" name of the

EXPERTS ONLY

document, remember, is the path.) Press Enter when you're done typing, and the list of files for that directory appears. More on directories later.

Using the Look Option

(Try before you buy)

Suppose that you can't find the file you want just by the name—a real dilemma if you don't use descriptive names. Have no fear. The Look option lets you peek at the file *before* you retrieve it.

First, highlight the name of the document that you *think* you want to work on. Then press Enter. The beginning of the document appears on-screen. You can use the arrow keys to move up and down through the document.

When you're finished looking at the file, press Enter again to go back to the List Files screen.

Checklist

▼ It's an almost overwhelming temptation to try to edit your document when you see it there in the Look screen. You can't. If you try, nothing will happen.

▼ If you're in the Look screen and find that you've picked the wrong file name, press N (for Next) to look at the next file or P (for Previous) to look at the previous file.

▼ The top of the Look screen tells you the name of the document you're looking at.

▼ Look is only good for looking at text files, and it's only really good for looking at WordPerfect files. If you try to look at files made by another word processor, Look will throw in some funny codes among the text. If you try to look at a graphics file or a program, Look will show you gobbledygook.

▼ Look gives you a pretty good idea of what your file contains, but if you're using fancy stuff in your files, like tables, columns, graphics, and fonts, they won't show up in Look.

▼ Exit the Look option by pressing F1.

Retrieving Documents without Using List Files

(Express delivery)

If you know the name of the document you want to retrieve, you don't have to dive into that cluttered List Files screen; you can retrieve the document from the comfort of your editing screen.

Here's how you retrieve a document:

1. Press Shift-F10.

At the bottom of the screen, the following message appears:

```
Document to be retrieved:  (List Files)
```

2. Type the name of the document you want to retrieve; then press Enter.

The document appears on-screen.

If you type the name of a file that doesn't exist, it prompts you with this message:

```
ERROR: File Not Found — your file name
```

TIP

Your screen won't actually show the words "your file name." This is just my way of saying that the screen will show the name of the file. The file name could be almost anything.

This message only lasts for a second or two, and then you're back to the `Document to be retrieved:` prompt. Try typing the name again, and be sure that you type it correctly. Or use List Files.

EXPERTS ONLY

What if I've put my file in another directory?

If you want to retrieve a document from somewhere other than the current directory, you have to type the path—the route to that document—and the document name at the Document to be retrieved: prompt. Suppose, for example, that you want to retrieve FUSION.CLD from your C:\SCIENCE\EXPERMNT\MAD directory. You would press Shift-F10, type **C:\SCIENCE\EXPERMNT\MAD\FUSION.CLD**, and press Enter.

After you retrieve the file, you can do any number of things: add text, change text, delete text, undelete text, or do the hokey-pokey and turn yourself around.

Formatting Essentials
(Looking Good)

IN A NUTSHELL

- ▼ Center a line
- ▼ Align text to the right margin
- ▼ Insert the current date
- ▼ Indent the first line of a paragraph
- ▼ Indent a whole paragraph
- ▼ Type **bold** text
- ▼ Type <u>underlined</u> text
- ▼ Type *italicized* text
- ▼ Add page numbers
- ▼ Double-space a document
- ▼ Take a peek at hidden codes

CHAPTER 5

There are hundreds of things you can do in WordPerfect to make documents look good. This chapter focuses on those that you'll use most often. After you master these few tricks, you can easily fake your way to a nice-looking letter or report.

Front and Center

To center a line on a typewriter, you need a doctorate in Mathematics: find the center of the page, count the number of characters in the title, divide by two, backspace that many times, cross your fingers, utter a few magic phrases, and type the title.

WordPerfect makes centering much easier. First, move your cursor to the line where you want to type the title. (This line should be blank.) Then press Shift-F6. Your cursor hops over to the center of the screen. Type your title and press Enter. The cursor moves back to the left margin.

Checklist

▼ If you've already typed your title and want to center it, move the cursor to the line that you want centered. Press Home, Home, left-arrow key to go to the beginning of the line. Then press Shift-F6.

▼ Pressing Shift-F6 is only for centering single-line titles. If you press Shift-F6, and then you type so much that your cursor jumps down a line, the second line of your title won't be centered.

▼ Chapter 10 tells you how to center multiple lines—even entire documents.

58

Aligning Text at the Right Margin

Another alignment choice in WordPerfect is right-alignment. For instance, you might like your dates or your return address aligned with the right margin. To align text to the right, press Alt-F6. Your cursor jumps to the right side of the page. Now start typing. As you type, the cursor stays at the right side of the screen and text moves to the left. Press Enter and the cursor moves back to the left margin.

Date Stamp

It's always a good idea to put the current date on letters you type. That way, people can grumble at the postal service—instead of you—when it takes them so long to receive their mail. Here's how you add the current date:

1. Move your cursor to a blank line.

This should be the line where you want the date to go.

2. Press Shift-F5 to bring up the Date menu.

3. Press T to insert the date.

4. Press Enter to go to the next line.

Checklist

▼ You can press Shift-F5, T anywhere in a document where you want the current date to appear; the date doesn't have to be on a line by itself.

continues

59

Checklist Continued

▼ You can do some other snazzy things with the Date feature. I'll keep you in suspense about them until Chapter 10.

Indenting Your Text

(To tab or indent: That is the question)

When people read your documents, visual cues help make reading easier. You may, for instance, want to indent the first line of each paragraph to show clearly where the paragraph starts. Or you may want to call attention to a particular paragraph by indenting the whole paragraph.

Use Tab to indent the first line of a paragraph

Use F4 to indent the whole paragraph

```
                       New TV Show Ideas
                     by Howard J. Beighfey

Build A Better You
     The American obsession with physical fitness wouldn't be so bad if
we didn't have to spend 72 hours per week in the weight room to achieve
the perfect body.  A qualified panel of biophysicists, biochemists, and other
scientists with the "bio" prefix will show you how—using everyday
drugstore chemicals—to concoct amazing fitness-giving potions. Sample
episodes might include:

     Stir together a few household cleansers and Presto! an enzyme that
     converts your recently-eaten double cheeseburger with bacon into a
     fibrous, celery-like substance.

     Whip up a chocolate shake containing a special acidic additive, and
     you've just performed a painless do-it-yourself liposuction.
     Give yourself a quick shot in the arm with your own home-made
     steroids, and watch the new you blossom in practically no time at all.

     Of course, the last ten minutes of each episode will be devoted to
engineering your own brand new, revved-up DNA right in your kitchen
sink.

C:\WP51\DATA\SCIENCE.9                          Doc 1 Pg 1 Ln 6" Pos 1.5"
```

Tabbing

To indent the first line of a paragraph, press Tab and type the paragraph. If you've already typed the paragraph, move the cursor to the beginning of the first line and press Tab. The first line will be indented one-half inch.

Indenting

To indent the entire paragraph, press F4 and then type the text. If you've already typed the text, move the cursor to the beginning of the paragraph and press F4. All lines in the paragraph will be indented one-quarter inch.

TIP

The Indent (F4) feature is great for making numbered lists. At the beginning of a line, type a list number and period, such as **1.** Then press F4. Type the text for the list item, and then press Enter. Repeat these steps for each item in the list. The numbers will line up with the margin, and the text will be indented.

Adding *Emphasis* to Your Text

(Make words scream for attention!)

One of the biggest disappointments of the written word is that you can't use hand and facial gestures. As I write this book, I'm waving my hands about and grimacing and occasionally sticking out my tongue. And you can't see any of it. Pity.

To show emotion in text, you can change the text style (or attribute) to **bold**, <u>underline</u>, and *italic*.

CAUTION

After you know how to use these emphasis tricks, you'll be tempted to use them all the time, and in combination. **<u>Don't</u>**. Too much emphasis defeats the purpose and makes your text look hyperactive.

Chapter 7 tells you how to emphasize text you've already typed.

Using Bold (Boldly going where no man has gone before)

Bold is great for titles and headings in your documents. It's not that great for emphasizing words in text. Use italic for words that need emphasis.

To type bold text, first move the cursor to where you want to place the bold text. Then press F6. F6 is the Bold key. When you turn on Bold, the number by Pos (in the lower right corner of the screen) changes color or turns bold.

Next, type the text.

Depending on the type of computer screen you have, the text you type will appear brighter than the ordinary text or will be a different color. This is WordPerfect's way of telling you that this text will be bold when you print the document.

When you're finished typing bold text, press F6. The same key that turns bold on turns it off.

Underlining Text

Back when typewriters were the writing tool of choice, underlined text was your only option. Most typewriters didn't have italic. My advice is to use italic rather than underline. Italic looks much nicer. If you <u>must</u> use underline, move the cursor to where you want to type the underlined text. Press F8 to turn on underline, and then begin typing. Your screen may show underlined text as underlined text, or it may show underlined text in a different color. Don't worry; the text will print underlined.

Press F8 again to turn off underline.

Italicizing Text (The elegant emphasis)

One surefire way to improve the look of your documents is to use italic as your main method of emphasizing text. *Italicized text stands out when you read it, without detracting from the overall look of the page.*

TIP

As with any emphasis, don't overuse italic. If you italicize too many words, your documents will be difficult to read.

Here is how you add italic text:

1. Move the cursor to where you want to begin typing italic text.

2. Press Ctrl-F8.

This key combo brings up the following menu of options:

```
1 Size; 2 Appearance; 3 Normal; 4 Base Font;
5 Print Color: 0
```

3. Press A for Appearance.

Yet another menu appears:

```
1 Bold 2 Undln 3 Dbl Und 4 Italc 5 Outln 6 Shadw
7 Sm Cap 8 Redln 9 Stkout: 0
```

4. Press I for Italc (which is WordPerfect talk for Italic).

Type your text. A few monitors actually show italic text on-screen; the rest either show it as underlined or a different color—yellow, for instance.

5. When you're done typing, press the right-arrow key to turn off italic.

Checklist

▼ You could also press Ctrl-F8, A, I to turn off italic the same way you turned it on, but why go to all the extra hassle? Pressing the right-arrow key does the same thing much more quickly.

▼ You can create a macro that turns on italic. Then you can perform the preceding steps simply by pressing a key combination. (A *macro* is a set of recorded keystrokes that can be replayed with a key combination. Chapter 19 covers the fascinating world of macros.)

Adding Page Numbers

Any time you type a document that is longer than a couple of pages, you probably want to number the pages. Typing the page numbers yourself isn't the answer—they'll get shifted around anytime you edit your document.

Whenever your document needs page numbers, use WordPerfect's Page Numbering feature. You can put the page numbers on the left, center, or right side of the page, and you can choose whether to put the page number on the top or bottom of the page. And if that's not enough, you can even alternate sides on even and odd pages.

This is how you tell WordPerfect to number the pages for you:

1. Press Home, Home, up-arrow key to move the cursor to the beginning of the document.

The cursor needs to be at the beginning of the document in order for the page numbering to begin on the first page.

2. Press Shift-F8 to bring up the Format menu.

3. Press P for Page.

Yet another menu shows up.

4. Press N for Page Numbering.

Yet another menu appears.

5. Press P for Page Number Position.

A series of three "boxes" appears on-screen. These boxes have numbers in them and represent pages. They show you the various places that page numbers can appear on the page.

6. Press one of the numbers, 1 through 8.

For example, if you want your page numbers to appear in the bottom center of each page, press 6, because 6 is in the bottom center of the "Every Page" box. If you want page numbers to appear in the outside corner of alternate pages, like they do in books, press 4 (for the top corner) or 8 (for the bottom corner).

```
Format: Page Number Position

      Every Page                    Alternating Pages
      ┌─────────────┐      ┌─────────────┐ ┌─────────────┐
      │ 1   2   3   │      │ 4           │ │           4 │
      │             │      │             │ │             │
      │             │      │ Even        │ │        Odd  │
      │             │      │             │ │             │
      │ 5   6   7   │      │ 8           │ │           8 │
      └─────────────┘      └─────────────┘ └─────────────┘

      9 - No Page Numbers




      Selection: 0
```

The Page Numbering menu.

When you press the option for the place you want your page numbers, you go back to a menu that reads `Format: Page Numbering`.

7. Press F7 to go back to the document screen.

▼ The page numbers don't appear in your on-screen document, but they will appear when you print the document. You can see them if you preview the document (which is covered in the next chapter).

▼ Shift-F8, the Format key, is the gateway to a plethora of features. So many, in fact, that Part III of this book talks of little else.

▼ Some writing styles dictate that the first page of letters and other documents shouldn't have a page number—instead, page numbering should start on the second page. If that's the way you work, move your cursor down so that it's on the second or third line of the first page—instead of the very top of the first page—before you follow the steps. Page numbering won't begin until the second page.

▼ If want the current page number somewhere in your document text, just press Ctrl-B where you want the current page number to appear. ^B appears on-screen. When you print the document, ^B will be replaced by the correct page number.

Changing Your Line Spacing

Sometimes you need double-spaced documents, sometimes you need 1 1/2 spacing, and so on. Changing line spacing isn't really all that hard. Here's how you do it:

1. Move the cursor to the place where you want the new line spacing to take effect.

2. Press Shift-F8 to bring up the Format menu.

3. Press L for Line.

4. Press S for Spacing.

Your cursor is on a line about midway down the screen. It looks like this:

```
6 - Line Spacing                    1
```

The number above your cursor is the line spacing that's in effect right now. You don't have to delete this number; it will disappear when you type a new one.

5. Type a number for the line spacing you want; then press Enter.

For example, if you want double spacing, type **2**; if you want 1 1/2 spacing, type **1.5**, and so forth.

6. Press F7 to return to your document.

This new line spacing is in effect from here to the end of the document, or to the next place you change line spacing.

Checklist

▼ Changed line spacing does show up on-screen. 1 1/2 spacing appears on-screen as double spacing. Not to worry; it will print correctly.

▼ You can have several line spacing changes in a single document, but it looks terrible. Your documents will look more consistent and professional if the line spacing does not change several times throughout.

TIP

Line spacing is the perfect feature to use if you need to subtly alter the length of your document. If you're supposed to have a three page paper and it only goes for 2 1/2 pages, go to the top of the document and change your line spacing to 1.3, instead of 1. The extra space between lines means an instant half page for you. You can make long-winded documents appear shorter in the same way—just decrease the line spacing.

Reveal Codes

(WordPerfect's sinister underworld)

Each time you make a formatting change, WordPerfect inserts a special code into your document. Most of the time, you don't even have to know the codes are there. But if your formatting starts to go haywire, you may need to travel to the Underworld where these hidden codes dwell.

To display the hidden codes, press Alt-F3.

The screen splits, and you see two versions of your document: the regular, normal document and the hidden, secretive codes that lurk below. Quickly press Alt-F3 again to turn off Reveal Codes.

Don't worry about Reveal Codes now. Chapter 12 helps you travel through this world to troubleshoot any formatting problems.

BUZZWORDS

REVEAL CODES

Reveal Codes are the hidden codes that WordPerfect inserts into your document for formatting changes. The codes can be singular (such as [Tab]) or can come in a set (such as [Bold On] and [Bold Off]). Usually you can guess from the name of the code what the code does.

CHAPTER 6

Printing Basics
(Getting It Down on Paper)

IN A NUTSHELL

▼ Use Print Preview
▼ Print a full document
▼ Print the current page

Y ou've really got to use your imagination when you're typing in WordPerfect. You can't see your page numbers or how the text will look on the page. You can't tell whether the lines are really centered or if the margins are right. You don't know for sure how the document will look on paper...until you see it on paper.

This chapter explains how to get a sneak preview of the document— display a close approximation of how it will look when printed. You also learn how to print a document.

Using Print Preview

(Coming soon to a printer near you)

When you're typing a document, it's difficult to tell how the final document will look. To really see the document—with all its special enhancements—you have to print it. Then you've got to make corrections, print it again, make more corrections, print it again, scream in frustration, print it again, develop an ulcer, print it again.

You can save a lot of time, frustration and trees by using the View Document feature. It gives you a good idea of how your document's going to look when it comes out of the printer, and it's much faster than printing your file.

To preview a page, move the cursor to the page you want to preview. Press Shift-F7, and then press V (for View document).

Depending on the speed of your computer, you may have to wait anywhere from 1 to 20 seconds for Print Preview to come on. (Be patient— this is serious magic at work.) Then, looking like a Polaroid snapshot of your page, up comes a preview of your document!

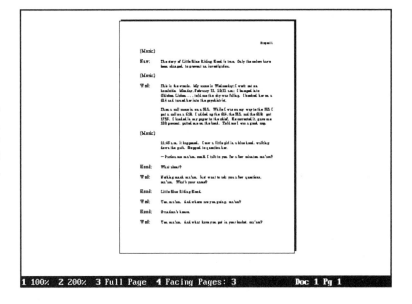

Press Shift-F7, V
to see a full-
page preview of
how a page will
look on paper.

Look at the View Document screen. Do you see any changes that you need to make to the document—center the footer, add the date, tighten up that seven-line title? When you're finished previewing the page, press F7 to go back to the document screen.

Checklist

▼ If the full-page view is too dinky for you to see details of your document, press 1 to change the view to 100%. You won't be able to see the whole page at a time, but you can see different parts of the page by pressing Home, and then the up- or down-arrow key.

▼ If you want to enlarge the view, press 2 for 200% magnification.

▼ If you're at the 100% or 200% magnification level and want to see the whole page again, press 3.

continues

▼ Press Page Up to view the previous page; press Page Down to go to the next page.

▼ If you want to jump to a certain page, press Ctrl-Home, type the page number you want (such as **15**), and press Enter.

"I HATE THIS!"

Nothing happens!

Suppose that you're at a document screen, you press Shift-F7, V, and nothing happens or you get a baffling error message. Any number of things could have caused the problem. You probably have a screen (monitor) that doesn't work with this feature. My advice is to call WordPerfect Customer Support (toll-free) at 800/541-5096 and tell them you can't get Print Preview to work. They'll be able to help you.

TIP

If everything in Print Preview looks good to you, you can print the document. Make sure that the printer is on and ready to print; then press F1, F.

Print the Entire Document

(I can't believe I printed the whole thing)

It's a great feeling to be finished with a document and ready to print. One of the few times people truly appreciate computers is when they see the results of their work on paper. But getting to that point isn't as easy as it sounds.

Turning On the Printer

Before you print your document, first make certain that your printer is turned on and ready to print. There are more than a thousand different types of printers, so there's not one set way to turn on a printer. Try flipping the biggest switch you can find on the printer. If something lights up, the printer is probably on. If nothing happens, be sure that the printer is plugged in. Or try a different switch.

You also might need to put the printer "on-line" (ready to go). Look for an On-Line button. If it's lit, you're probably OK. If it's not, try pressing it. If there isn't one, you probably don't need to put the printer on-line.

If you can't get the printer on and on-line, put on your best pathetic face and ask some computer-savvy friend to help you.

Printing the Document

Next,retrieve the document you want to print (if it's not on-screen already). Chapter 4 covers the delicacies of retrieving a document. After the document is on-screen, you're set to go. Press Shift-F7, and then press F (for Full Document).

Your document begins printing.

"I HATE THIS!"

My printer won't print

There is a veritable cornucopia of reasons why your document may not print. Sometimes it's the computer's fault, sometimes it's the printer's fault, sometimes it's the fault of the cable that connects the two, sometimes it's the fault of WordPerfect, and sometimes it's the fault of Congress. Solving printing problems is one of the hardest things you can

"I HATE THIS!"

do in WordPerfect, and I suggest you try to get somebody else—the local WordPerfect guru or a WordPerfect Customer Service Rep—to go through the grief.

After you press Shift-F7, F and WordPerfect goes back to the document screen, you're free to get back to work. You can continue typing, editing—whatever. WordPerfect will continue to print. In fact, there's no reason for the document to even be on-screen anymore. You can go ahead and clear it; WordPerfect will print it just the same.

CAUTION

If you do try to work while WordPerfect is printing, don't use View Document. For some reason, WordPerfect can't print and use View Document at the same time. If you do go into View Document while you're trying to print a document, WordPerfect will wait until you come back out before it finishes the print job.

CAUTION

Don't exit WordPerfect or turn off the computer until all your print jobs are finished printing. Although you can keep working while a document is printing, the document will not continue printing if you exit WordPerfect or turn off your computer.

Print the Current Page

(One at a time, please)

You might want to print a single page—not the whole document. To print a single page from the document you're working on, first make sure that your printer's ready to go. Then:

1. Move the cursor to anywhere on the page you want to print.

Use your Page Up/Page Down keys to move quickly from page to page.

2. Press Shift-F7 to bring up the Print menu.

3. Press P to print the page.

WordPerfect takes you back to the document screen and you can get back to work.

PART II

The On-Line Editorial Assistant

Includes:

CHAPTER 7

Handling Big Chunks of Your Document

IN A NUTSHELL

▼ Highlight text
▼ Delete highlighted text
▼ Move highlighted text
▼ Make copies of high-lighted text
▼ Save highlighted text as its own file
▼ Print highlighted text
▼ Make highlighted text bold, underlined, or italic
▼ Alphabetize highlighted text

CHAPTER 7

I f you've ever drawn a circle around a paragraph and then made an arrow from the circle to where the paragraph should go, you already understand the idea behind WordPerfect's Block feature. And if you don't, I'll tell you.

The idea behind WordPerfect's Block feature is to highlight a chunk of text, and then do something with it. This chapter shows you the ways you can highlight a block of text, and then it shows you what you can do with the block.

Blocking Text

(The electronic highlighter)

Blocking refers to highlighting (selecting) a chunk (block) of text—a word, line, paragraph, whatever. After you highlight the block, you can do just about anything with it: make it bold, move it to a different page, and much, much more!

You can use one of two methods to block text: the arrow keys or the mouse.

Block Text by Using the Arrow Keys

The easiest way to highlight text is with the arrow keys. First, move the cursor to where you want to begin the block. The cursor should be right under the first letter you want in the block. Then press Alt-F4. Word-Perfect lets you know that Block is on by showing the following at the bottom left of the screen:

```
Block On
```

Use the arrow keys to move the cursor after the last character you want in the block. As you move the cursor, everything between the starting point of your block and your current position is highlighted.

```
      Jill's day started out bad and then got worse. First, she
woke up with the theme to Jeopardy running endlessly through her
head. Do-do-do-do, do-do-do, do-do-do-do-DO, do, do, do, do. No
matter how hard she shook her head, she couldn't get the song
out.
      Then something worse happened. Everything that came out of
her mouth was in the phrase of a question.




Block on                                    Doc 1 Pg 1 Ln 1.33" Pos
```

Highlighted (blocked) text

Checklist

▼ If you want to block a sentence, the cursor should wind up to the right of the period, not under it.

▼ If you've got a section of text blocked, and then decide you don't want to block text after all, press F1 to turn off Block.

▼ Besides using your arrow keys, you can use the other cursor-movement keys to highlight text. For example, after Block is on, you can block to the end of the document by pressing Home, Home, down-arrow key.

▼ If you've got an F12 key, press it to turn on Block. This takes less finger-stretching than pressing Alt-F4.

TIP

When you turn on Block, you're automatically in Instant Search mode. That means that WordPerfect will jump to the next character you press. You can use this tip to highlight text quickly.

First, move your cursor to where you want the block to begin. Press Alt-F4 to turn on Block. Then press the character you want the block to jump to. For example, if you want to jump to the end of the sentence, you could press the period (.). WordPerfect would move the cursor *after* the next period it finds. If you want to block the next two sentences, press the period twice (..).

Block Text by Using the Mouse

Although the mouse is basically lifeless in WordPerfect, it does a great job blocking text. Use the mouse to move the mouse pointer (a little rectangle that doesn't appear until you move the mouse) on-screen so that it's directly over the first character you want in the block.

"I HATE THIS!"

I'm moving my mouse, but nothing happens

If you can't see a mouse pointer moving around when you use the mouse, WordPerfect isn't set up to work with your mouse. Find a WordPerfect guru to help you get it working.

Press and hold down the left mouse button. While holding down the mouse button, move the mouse so that the pointer is where you want the end of the block.

As you move the mouse, text is highlighted. If you move the mouse pointer so that it's at the bottom of the screen, text scrolls up. When the text is highlighted, let go of the mouse button.

Deleting a Block of Text

If you don't like something you've written, you don't have to scribble through it. Instead, block the text to be annihilated. Then press Backspace. WordPerfect asks

```
Delete Block? No (Yes)
```

Press Y for Yes. The block is gone.

Checklist

▼ If you decide you didn't want to delete the text after all, press F1, R to restore the text you just deleted.

▼ Deleting a block of text can also be used as a tricky way to move your information. Just delete the block of text you want to move, and then move your cursor to where you want to insert the text. Press F1, R to place the text in its new home. WordPerfect remembers only the three most-recent deletions, so make sure that you restore the deleted text right away.

Moving Text

As you write documents, you'll probably notice from time to time that a certain sentence would make more sense a couple of paragraphs later, or your introduction works better as a conclusion. And hey, wouldn't point C be clearer if it came between points A and B?

WordPerfect lets you freely juggle blocks of text. Here's how:

1. Highlight the text you want to move.

2. Press Ctrl-F4 (the Move key), B to choose Block, and then M to choose Move.

The block of text disappears. This is called *cutting* because you snipped a chunk of text right out of your document—just as if you had used scissors.

The following prompt appears at the bottom of the screen:

```
Move cursor; press Enter to retrieve.
```

3. Move the cursor to where you want to insert the block of text and press Enter.

The block of text is *pasted* in its new place.

Checklist

▼ WordPerfect holds your text in its memory until you cut another block of text or exit WordPerfect. Make sure that you *paste* (put) the text into a new position in the document before you exit WordPerfect. If you don't, the text will be gone forever.

▼ After you've cut text, you can paste it as many times into as many places as you like. To paste text again, press Shift-F10, Enter.

▼ You may need to go to the beginning or end of the pasted text and put in some spaces or hard returns (which you make by pressing Enter) to make it look right.

Copy Cat Text

Suppose that you want to use the same text more than once. You want the original to stay put where it is, but you want to use that same block of text again somewhere else. That's called *copying and pasting*, and this is how you do it:

1. Block the text you want to copy.

2. Press Ctrl-F4 (the Move key), B for Block, and C for Copy.

The highlighting disappears, but a copy of the block is safely tucked away in WordPerfect's memory. The screen now shows this prompt:

```
Move cursor; press Enter to retrieve.
```

3. Move the cursor to where you want to place a copy of your block of text; then press Enter.

The prompt disappears and your block appears.

▼ WordPerfect holds your text in its memory until you cut another block of text or exit WordPerfect. Make sure that you *paste* (put) the text into a new position in the document before you exit WordPerfect. If you don't, the text will be gone forever.

▼ After you've copied text, you can paste it as many times into as many places as you like. To paste text again, press Shift-F10, Enter.

▼ You may need to go to the beginning or end of the pasted text and put in some spaces or hard returns (which you make by pressing Enter) to make it look right.

Saving Text You Use All the Time

Chances are, you often say the same stuff over and over in a document— particularly in letters. You can save part of a document and then insert that part into another document. For instance, you might get tired of typing the following:

> We are sorry that your Roy Orbison wig caught fire. We thought we had thoroughly tested the wig's flammability. Please accept our sincere apologies and this coupon for $5 off our Liberace wig.

You can save this block of text and use it again and again. It's a two-step process: save the text in a new file, insert the text.

Saving the Text

To save the text, block the part of the document you want to save as its own file. Then press F10. You see this prompt at the bottom of the screen:

```
Block name:
```

Type a name for the document (the block); then press Enter. Make sure that you follow the rules for document names—eight letters or fewer, with an optional period and three more letters. No spaces. (Take a look at the section "The Name Game" in Chapter 3 for more details about naming files.)

After the block of text has been saved, the text is no longer highlighted.

Inserting the Saved Text

To put that saved block of text into another document, move the cursor to where you want the block, press Shift-F10, type the name you gave the block, and press Enter.

Print a Block of Text

(Prints Charming)

If you've just written a couple of paragraphs and want a chance to take an old-fashioned red pen to them, you don't have to print the whole document. You can print just the part you need. Make sure that your printer is turned on and ready to print. Guess what you do next? Did you guess that you have to block the part of the document you want to print?

Congratulations. You're getting the hang of it.

After you block the text, press Shift-F7. This prompt comes up:

```
Print block? No (Yes)
```

Press Y for Yes. The block prints—right in the same position as it would've if you had printed the whole page. Headers, page numbers, and other gadgets like that are printed, too.

Adding Oomph to Blocked Text

If you really want to make a section of text stand out, make it bold or italic or underlined.

First, block the text that you want to emphasize. Then do one of the following:

▼ Press F6 to make the blocked text **bold**.

▼ Press F8 to <u>underline</u> it.

▼ Press Ctrl-F8, A, I to make it *italic*.

The text takes on the appearance that you applied, and Block is turned off.

TIP

You can block the text again by pressing Alt-F4, Ctrl-Home, Ctrl-Home. If you want, you can *really* emphasize the text by adding another emphasizer—***bold italic***, for example.

Alphabetizing Text

Alphabetizing text is a sort of quasi-block function. It will come in handy when you need to sort something like a list of names. First, save your document. Sorting isn't *that* dangerous, but if the sort does come out wrong, you can go always back to the original.

Next, block the list of names. Then press Ctrl-F9; a funky screen appears. This is the Sort screen, the complexity of which has driven many people completely mad. Avert your eyes and press P quickly. The list is sorted by the first word in each line.

Any guidelines about sorting lists? Glad you asked

▼ Each list item should only be one line long. This kind of alphabetizing doesn't work with list items that take two or more lines.

▼ Each item should end with a hard return (press Enter).

▼ Don't block any part of the document that isn't part of the list. For example, if there's an introduction before the actual listing of the names, that introduction shouldn't be included.

"I HATE THIS!"

What about all those Smiths?

If two lines have the same first word, they may not be alphabetized by the second word. There are ways to fix this problem, but that would be a subject best covered in one of those big, nasty, heavy books. Ask a WordPerfect guru for help.

THIS BEEPING PILE OF PLASTIC JUST AIN'T A TYPEWRITER.

BY JEFF MACNELLY

WHERE'S THE DING?

IN THE GOOD OLD DAYS OF NEWSPAPERING YOUR TRUSTY TYPEWRITER WOULD HELP YOU EXPRESS YOURSELF...

YOU COULD POUND THE KEYS HARDER WHEN YOU WERE MAD...

AND PLAY THAT UNDERWOOD LIKE A PIANO WHEN YOU FELT POETIC.

MOST IMPORTANT, THOUGH, WAS THE WAY YOU COULD BLOW OFF STEAM WHEN YOU MADE A MISTAKE...

TAPPA... TAPPA... TAPPA... PATTA...

YOU COULD RIP OUT THE PAPER, CRUMPLE IT UP AND HEAVE IT ACROSS THE NEWSROOM.

ZIP!

SOMEHOW IT MADE YOU FEEL A LOT BETTER WHEN YOU DID THAT...

BUT TODAY, WITH THESE WORD PROCESSORS AND COMPUTERS,... WELL, IT JUST AIN'T THE SAME...

BUT IT'S STILL PRETTY SATISFYING.

10/9

CHAPTER 8

Using WordPerfect's Dictionary and Thesaurus
(Getting It Right)

IN A NUTSHELL

- ▼ Check the spelling in your document
- ▼ Check the spelling in a single page
- ▼ Check the spelling in a block
- ▼ Look up a word
- ▼ Add new words to WordPerfect's dictionary
- ▼ Find how many words are in your document
- ▼ Find synonyms for words
- ▼ Find antonyms for words

CHAPTER 8

Y ou spell potatoe, I spell potato. Ex-Vice President jokes aside, most of us are lousy spellers. And the few of us who are gifted with spelling make typos anyway. It comes down to this: we all make spelling mistakes.

WordPerfect can be a real lifesaver when it comes to checking your work for spelling errors. WordPerfect can look through your document and flag any possible mistakes; then it lets you decide how to correct them. You can also polish your writing by finding *precisely* the word you need with WordPerfect's Thesaurus.

Checking Your Spelling

(I before E except after C)

There's nothing more embarrassing than a big glaring misspelling in a document. You can try to convince everyone that it was a careless typo, but they'll always think you spell "Marine Corps" "Marine Core."

To avoid the embarrassment, check your spelling. First make sure that the document you want to check is on-screen. If you want to check the entire document, don't worry about the position of the cursor. Word-Perfect starts at the beginning of a document and works its way to the end.

If you want to check the spelling on a certain page only, move your cursor so that it's anywhere on that page.

Next press Ctrl-F2 to start checking spelling. This prompt appears at the bottom of the screen:

```
Check: 1 Word; 2 Page; 3 Document; 4 New Sup. Dictionary;
5 Look Up; 6 Count: 0
```

Press D to check all the text in your document, or P to check the current page.

After WordPerfect finds a word that it thinks is misspelled, it highlights the word and shows a list of possible corrections. A bar divides the top half of the screen from the bottom. The top half of the screen shows your document; the bottom half is reserved for showing possible corrections for misspelled words.

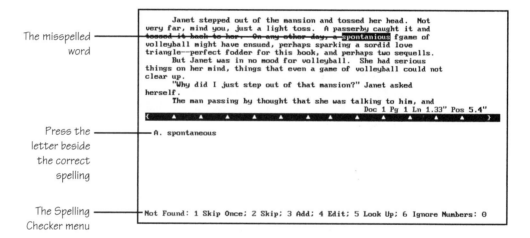

The misspelled word

Press the letter beside the correct spelling

The Spelling Checker menu

After you make a correction, WordPerfect moves to the next misspelling.

Correcting Mistakes

You have lots of choices about how to handle a word that WordPerfect flags:

CHAPTER 8

Checklist

▼ If the correct spelling is listed in the bottom half of the screen, press the letter beside the correct spelling. Suppose, for example, that *spontanious* is highlighted and the bottom of the screen shows:

        A. spontaneous

Press A to replace the misspelled word with the correct spelling.

▼ WordPerfect doesn't know every word in the world. When it comes across a word it doesn't know—like a name or a specialized term you use—WordPerfect highlights the word and assumes that it's spelled wrong. If you plan to use that word frequently, you can add it to WordPerfect's dictionary by pressing 3 (for Add). From now on, WordPerfect will know the word and won't flag it as being misspelled.

▼ If WordPerfect stops on a word it shouldn't, but you don't want to add the word to the dictionary, press 2. WordPerfect will ignore the word for the rest of the spelling check. You can also have WordPerfect skip the word just once by pressing 1, but I can't think of any reasons you would want to do that.

▼ If WordPerfect stops on a misspelled word but none of its suggestions are what you want, press 4 for Edit. Your cursor jumps up to the misspelled word and you can fix the mistake yourself. When you're done, press F7 to tell WordPerfect to start checking again.

▼ WordPerfect thinks any word with a number in it is wrong. If you use words that contain numbers, press 6 to turn off number checking.

Double Double Words

If you have the same word twice in a row (such as "up up and away!"), WordPerfect counts that as a problem, too. The two words are highlighted and you see this prompt:

```
Double Word: 1 2 Skip; 3 Delete 2nd; 4 Edit; 5 Disable
Double Word Checking
```

You can ignore the double word by pressing 1 or 2. You can get rid of one of the occurrences of the word by pressing 3. If you want to tidy things up yourself, press 4, do your editing, and press F7 to get back to checking your spelling. If you want WordPerfect to ignore double words, press 5 (but I wouldn't do that if I were you).

wRONG cASE

WordPerfect even checks to see whether you've gone a little crazy with your Shift key. If you've got unusual punctuation in a word, such as the first two letters being capitalized, WordPerfect shows you this prompt:

```
Irregular Case: 1 2 Skip; 3 Replace; 4 Edit; 5 Disable
Case Checking
```

Pressing 1 or 2 makes WordPerfect skip past the word, 3 makes Word-Perfect change the word to more ordinary punctuation. If you press 4, the cursor goes to the word and lets you fix things yourself. Press F7 when you're ready to continue checking spelling. Press 5 if you want WordPerfect to stop looking for unusual capitalization.

Stop the Speller

If you decide to stop checking your spelling before WordPerfect's done, press F1 for Cancel. At the bottom of the screen, WordPerfect reports the number of words it's checked so far. Press F1 again to make the prompt disappear.

The Spell Check is Finished

When WordPerfect has finished, it shows a prompt like this:

```
Word count: 1620        Press any key to continue
```

If you need to know how many words are in that page or document (depending on which you checked), make a note of the number.

Press Enter (or any other key that strikes your fancy) to make the prompt go away.

Things to Hate about the Speller

WordPerfect's Speller isn't perfect. Here are a couple things it won't do:

Checklist

▼ WordPerfect's "dictionary" is really nothing more than a long list of words. If you want a definition of a word, you're going to have to get out the old-fashioned paper dictionary and look up the word.

▼ WordPerfect is not a proofreader. When WordPerfect checks your spelling, it only looks for correctly spelled words. It has no way of telling whether you used the words in the right way. If you write "pane" where you should write "pain," WordPerfect won't see a problem because the word is spelled correctly. So, use WordPerfect to check *you're* spelling, but make sure you *reed* your document carefully *two* make sure it makes *cents*.

TIP

There are programs designed to check your grammar. Que (the publishers of the book you are reading this very second) makes one of these grammar checkers, called RightWriter. Buy it. It's good.

Spelling Check Shortcuts

You don't have to check the entire document. If you've checked a document before and have just added a paragraph, you can check just that paragraph. Or you might want to check just one word.

To check a block of text, press Alt-F4; then move your cursor to where you want the spelling check to end. The section you want to check is highlighted. Press Ctrl-F2 to start the Speller. WordPerfect checks only the block.

To check just one word, move the cursor so that it's on the word you want to check, press Ctrl-F2 to start the Speller, and then press W (for Word). If you got the word right, WordPerfect doesn't do anything but

move the cursor to the next word. If you got the word wrong, WordPerfect highlights the word and shows some suggestions. Make a change and then press F1 to leave the Speller.

Looking Up a Word

There are certain words people just cannot remember how to spell. *Definitely* is definately one of them. If you need to write a word that you just don't know how to spell, you can look it up. Here's how:

1. Press Ctrl-F2.

This prompt appears:

```
Check: 1 Word; 2 Page; 3 Document; 4 New Sup. Dictionary;
5 Look Up; 6 Count: 0
```

2. Press L to look up a word.

Another prompt appears:

```
Word or word pattern:
```

3. Type your best guess for the word; then press Enter.

But how are you supposed to try to type a word you don't know how to spell? Just take a wild guess. WordPerfect will then take a couple of guesses at what it thinks you meant to type.

4. Write down the correct spelling. Unfortunately, WordPerfect won't let you place the word directly into your document. You have to type it in.

5. Press F1 twice to return to the document screen.

TIP

If you really have no idea how part of the word is spelled, just put an asterisk (*) in place of that part. The asterisk means "I'm not sure how this chunk of the word is spelled." Suppose that you need to use the word *hematophagous* (and I hope you never do) but don't have a clue what comes between the *hem* and the *us*. Just press Ctrl-F2, L; type **hem*us**; and press Enter. Among several other very obscure words, *hematophagous* shows up.

EXPERTS ONLY

Cheating at crossword puzzles

Yes, you can use WordPerfect's spelling checker to cheat at crossword puzzles. If you know how long the word should be and know at least a couple of its letters, you can probably get WordPerfect to figure out the rest.

To use the Cheat-At-A-Crossword-Puzzle feature, press Ctrl-F2, L (for Look Up). Type the word you need, using a question mark for every letter you don't know. For instance, if you need a nine-letter word for indigestion and you know "d" is the first letter, "e" is the fifth and "i" is the eighth, you would type **d???e??i?**. This is called a word *pattern*.

After you've typed the pattern, press Enter. WordPerfect lists all the words it knows that fit into the pattern you've set—including *dyspepsia*. If there are more words that fit the pattern than will fit on-screen, you can press Enter to see another screenful of words.

CHAPTER 8

EXPERTS ONLY

> When you're done, you're ready to cheat at another word by typing its pattern, or you can go back to your document by pressing F1 twice.

Counting Words

(Something to do when your computer can't sleep at night)

Some fussy college professors, bosses, and publishing houses like to know *exactly* how many words your document contains. If you're not a word-counter, skip this section. If, on the other hand, you need to know the number of words that your documents contain, read on. WordPerfect can easily accommodate you.

First, have the document on-screen. It doesn't matter where the cursor is positioned—top, bottom, middle, it's all the same to WordPerfect.

Next, press Ctrl-F2. The Speller main menu appears. Press C (for Count).

You'll have to wait for a little while WordPerfect counts all the words in your document. WordPerfect tells you to `* Please Wait *`. When it's finished counting, WordPerfect shows a prompt at the bottom of the screen:

```
Word count: 1620        Press any key to continue
```

Press F1 twice to return to the document screen.

Finding the Right Word

If you've ever stared blankly at your computer for ten minutes, wishing you could come up with the perfect word, WordPerfect's Thesaurus may be just the brainstorming tool you need. The Thesaurus gives you a list of *synonyms* (words that have the same—or at least similar—meaning) for a selected word. This same feature also lists *antonyms*, words with the opposite meaning as what you pick.

To find a synonym or antonym for a word in your document, move the cursor so that it's under the word you want to check. Then press Alt-F1 to start the Thesaurus feature.

A box with three columns appears at the bottom of the screen. The word you're looking up is highlighted at the top of the screen, and a series of synonyms appears in the columns. Depending on how many synonyms WordPerfect knows, the words may fill more than one column. After the synonyms comes a separator line; then any antonyms are listed. The synonyms and antonyms are divided into groups, which are numbered.

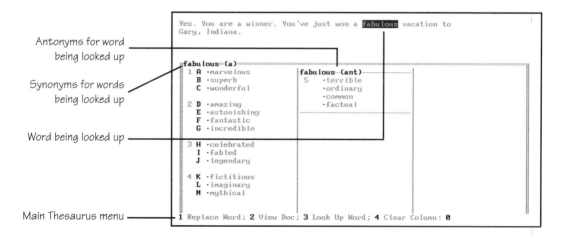

Antonyms for word being looked up

Synonyms for words being looked up

Word being looked up

Main Thesaurus menu

"I HATE THIS!"

What's a synonym for 'moronic'?

WordPerfect doesn't know synonyms or antonyms for every word. If it doesn't have any suggestions, WordPerfect will flash Word Not Found for a second, then give you a chance to look up a different word. You can press F1 to turn off the Thesaurus, or look up a different word by typing a word and pressing Enter.

Replacing the Word

If you see a word you like better in the replacement list, make sure that a letter is by the word you want to use. (You can make this group of letters move into a different column by pressing the left- and right-arrow keys.) Then press 1 for Replace Word.

This prompt appears:

```
Press letter for word
```

Press the letter corresponding to the word you want. The Thesaurus box disappears and you can get back to writing.

To leave the Thesaurus without picking any words, press F1 until the Thesaurus columns disappear.

CAUTION

Don't take WordPerfect's word for it! If WordPerfect says a word is a synonym for a word you're looking up, but you're not very familiar with the word, look it up in the dictionary. Make sure that it means what you need it to mean.

Looking Up Synonyms of the Synonyms

You can look up synonyms—and antonyms—of the words that are in the Thesaurus columns. Use the arrow keys to move the group of letters so that it's in the column containing the word you want to look up and press the letter beside the word. A column containing synonyms and antonyms for the word appears.

Checklist

▼ If a word doesn't have a dot by it, don't bother to try to look it up; WordPerfect doesn't have any synonyms or antonyms for it.

▼ If you fill up all three columns, you can clean up the screen. Move the group of letters to a column containing words you don't need, and then press 4 for Clear Column.

▼ If you want to look up a word that isn't in your text, press Alt-F1, 4 to clear out the Thesaurus columns, press 3 to look up a word, type the word you want to check for synonyms, and then press Enter.

CHAPTER 9

Finding and Replacing Text

(The WordPerfect Swap Meet)

IN A NUTSHELL

- ▼ Find a word
- ▼ Find formatting "codes"
- ▼ Replace one word or phrase with another—one at a time
- ▼ Replace one word or phrase with another in one fell swoop

Suppose that you are at the end of a long chapter in your novel and you can't remember the fate of Aunt Matilda. Something happened to mean, old Aunt Matilda somewhere in the chapter, but you can't remember where or what. Did they find the dead man in her cellar and give her the electric chair? Or did she escape on a motorcycle?

WordPerfect's Search feature can help with these types of dilemmas. Rather than read through the entire chapter, you can use the Search feature to look for specific text—such as *Matilda*—in your documents.

WordPerfect's companion feature, Replace, is another great editing tool. Suppose that your real Aunt Matilda calls and says that on second thought, she *is* going to include you in her will. You better change all references from mean, old Aunt Matilda to mean, old Aunt Helga. You can do so with Replace.

Searching for Text

(Where, oh where, has my little text gone?)

Use Search whenever you need to find a certain word or phrase. The search begins from your cursor and stops when it finds the text you need. You can search backward or forward through the document. Here's how you search for specific text:

1. Move the cursor to wherever you want to begin the search.

TIP

If you want to search through all the text in the document, press Home, Home, up-arrow key before you begin the search. This moves the cursor to the top of the document.

2. Press F2 to search through text that comes after the cursor, or Shift-F2 to search through text that comes before the cursor.

If you press F2, you see this at the bottom of the screen:

```
-> Srch:
```

Take another look at the arrow (->) in the prompt. The arrow's job is to tell you which way WordPerfect will be searching. Because the arrow is pointing right, WordPerfect will search forward—from the cursor toward the end of your document.

If you press Shift-F2, you get almost the same prompt, but the arrow points the other way, like this: <-. This tells you that WordPerfect's going to search from the cursor toward the beginning of the document.

3. Type the word or phrase you want WordPerfect to find. *Don't press Enter.*

The word or phrase you're typing is called the *search text.* It's best to type the search text in lowercase letters, even if you want to search for a proper name. If you're one of those inquisitive types who wants to know why, read the Experts Only section "The strange-but-true reason you should type search text in lowercase."

4. Press F2 to begin the search. (It doesn't matter whether you are searching forward or backward. You still press F2 here.)

WordPerfect searches through your document until it finds the text you're looking for. The cursor then stops to the right of that text.

TIP

After you find the text you're looking for, you may want to look for the next time it appears in the document. Press F2, F2. To find the previous occurrence, press Shift-F2, F2.

Rules of the hunt

▼ If WordPerfect can't find the text you want, * Not Found * flashes at the bottom of the screen for a moment, and then disappears. If you get a * Not Found * message and you're sure the text is there, try again. Make sure that you're typing exactly what you're looking for. Don't add any extra spaces or punctuation at the end of the word. If you still get a * Not Found * message, try searching in the other direction.

▼ If you press F2 or Shift-F2 and text from a previous search appears, just type the new text. The old text will disappear.

▼ You can change the direction of the search even after you've started typing the text you want to search for. Just press the up-arrow key if you want to search from the cursor up through the document, or press the down-arrow key if you want to search down through the document.

▼ If you press F2 or Shift-F2, and then decide you don't want to search after all, press F1 to go back to the document screen.

▼ If the text you want to find is in a header, footer, footnote, or endnote, this process won't find it. See the Experts Only section "What if the text is in some strange place like a header?"

110

▼ If you are searching for a single word, type a space before and after the word. Otherwise, WordPerfect will stop on every instance of the word that it finds. In other words, if you tell WordPerfect to find *it* and you don't include spaces before and after the word, WordPerfect will stop on *bandit*, *intuition*, and any other word that contains the letters *it*.

"I HATE THIS!"

Don't press Enter to start the search!

One of the easiest mistakes to make when searching for text is to press Enter after you type the search text. Pressing Enter doesn't start the search. Instead, it enters a hard return code ([HRt]) in the search text and tells WordPerfect to find the text followed by an [HRt] code. (The next section covers formatting codes.) If this happens, press Backspace to delete the code. Then press F2.

EXPERTS ONLY

The strange-but-true reason you should type search text in lowercase

When WordPerfect searches for text, it matches lowercase letters to both lowercase and uppercase letters. So if you type **nacho** as your search text, WordPerfect would think *nacho*, *Nacho*, *NACHO*, or anything in between is a match and would stop.

If you use uppercase letters as part of your search string, though, WordPerfect only matches them to other uppercase letters. If your search text were **Frijole**, WordPerfect would count *Frijole* or *FRIJOLE* as a match, since both words have capital F's. However, *frijole* would not count as a match, because it doesn't have a capital F.

CHAPTER 9

EXPERTS ONLY

What if the text is in some strange place like a header?

When you do a normal search, WordPerfect just hunts through the regular text. It doesn't look at headers, footers, footnotes, and endnotes. If you want to include these text elements in your search, plus all the regular text, you need to do what WordPerfect calls an *extended search*. To do an extended search, press Home, F2 rather than just F2.

If the text you want is in a header, footer, or some other fancy part of the program, WordPerfect will take you right to it. This means that when the search is done, you'll be sitting who-knows-where. After you've done what you need to do, press F7 until you get back to the document screen.

Searching for Formatting Codes

You can also search for WordPerfect *formatting codes*, which are the things that make your text look the way it does. (The wacky world of formatting is covered in Part III of this book.)

For example, if you want to search for the next place bold is turned on, press F2 to bring up the `-> Srch:` prompt; then press F6—the Bold key—to tell WordPerfect that you want to search for something bold. When you press F6, `[BOLD]` appears at the cursor. Press F2 to begin the search. WordPerfect stops at the first bold text it finds.

You can search for other formatting things, like tabs, Enters, line spacing changes, and so forth. Press F2 or Shift-F2, press the keystrokes you would use to turn on the feature you're searching for, and then press F2 again.

Using the Replace Feature

(Pulling the ole switcharoo)

Say that you've been working on a letter about toxic waste to President Bush. (You're against it.) Before you add the finishing touches, the election changes the whole political scene and makes your letter outdated. Do you have to retype the letter?

Not with WordPerfect's Replace feature. The Replace feature is perfect for making wholesale changes to your documents. You can use it to change every instance of a word or phrase into another, or you can pick and choose which instances to change.

CAUTION

After WordPerfect has gone through your document and replaced all the old text, the replacement can't be undone. Just in case you get results you don't want, always save your document before using the Replace feature. That way, if Replace changes things you didn't want to change, you can clear the screen and retrieve the file as it was before the ill-fated Replace operation. For steps on saving, clearing, and retrieving documents, see Chapters 3 and 4.

TIP

It's a good idea to start by replacing text one incident at a time. That way, you can be sure that the search is going as planned. You don't want to turn a search and replace into a search-and-destroy mission.

Replacing One by One

You might not want WordPerfect to go hog-wild and automatically re-place *every* instance of a word or phrase with another. For example, suppose that in your letter to the president you include the sentence "I'm tired of being relegated to the bush leagues." If you did a blanket Search and Replace, WordPerfect would change this sentence to "I'm tired of being relegated to the clinton leagues."

Instead, you might choose to give it the ole thumbs-up to replace the text after each incident that it finds of the text. Here's how:

1. Move the cursor to where you want to begin replacing text. You will generally want to begin at the top of the document; you can move there by pressing Home, Home, up-arrow key.

2. Press Alt-F2 to turn on the Replace feature. The following prompt appears:

   ```
   w/Confirm? No (Yes)
   ```

3. Press Y so that WordPerfect *will* ask each time it wants to replace something. A different prompt appears:

   ```
   -> Srch:
   ```

4. Type the text you want to replace; then press F2. For your letter, you would type **bush**, which is the text that needs to be replaced.

   Now this prompt appears:

   ```
   Replace with:
   ```

5. Type the *replacement text*; then press F2. For the letter, type **clinton**. That's the text you want to insert in place of the text in step 4.

WordPerfect stops each time it finds your search text and displays the following prompt:

```
Confirm? No (Yes)
```

6. Press Y if you want to replace the text. Press N if you want to leave this instance alone.

WordPerfect continues on, looking for the next instance of the text you want to replace. When it's found all of them, the prompts go away and you can go back to work.

CAUTION

> If you get partially through the Replace process and decide you want to stop, press F1. Remember, though, that the replacements that have already been made will remain changed.

Replacing Text in One Fell Swoop

If you are sure, absolutely sure, you want to make all the replacements without verifying them, press N when WordPerfect asks w/ `Confirm?` (This is step 3 in the preceding set of steps.) WordPerfect replaces each instance of your search text with your replacement text. It doesn't ask you first.

Replacement Tips

Here are some ideas on how to get the most from the Replace feature:

▼ The Replace feature is terrific for cleaning up irregular capitalization in documents. For example, if you sometimes forget to capitalize *American*, you can fix the problem in one pass. For the search text, type the word in lowercase (**american**). For the replacement text, type the word with its correct capitalization (**American**).

▼ Your documents will look their best if you have only one space at the end of each sentence. (Two spaces at the end of each sentence went out with the typewriter.) You can get rid of those habitual extra spaces using the Replace feature. For the search text, press the space bar twice. For the replacement text, press it once.

▼ If the text you want to replace is in a funky place (header, footer, footnote, endnote), press Home, Alt-F2 in step 2. WordPerfect will then include this text in the search.

▼ You can use the Replace feature to remove all instances of a word or phrase, replacing the word or phrase with nothing. For the replacement text, just press F2 instead of typing anything.

▼ If you want to replace text in a certain part of your document, move the cursor to the beginning of that part, press Alt-F4, and then move the cursor to the end of the section. After the section is selected (*blocked*), use Replace as you normally would. Only text in the block will be replaced. (Chapter 7 tells you all about the Block feature.)

PART III

Formatting Essentials

Includes:

CHAPTER 10

WordPerfect Formatting Features You'll Use Every Day

IN A NUTSHELL

- ▼ Use Tab to indent the first line of a paragraph
- ▼ Indent a paragraph
- ▼ Center text
- ▼ Align text along the right margin
- ▼ Add emphasis to your text by making it bold, underlined, or italic
- ▼ Choose exotic, exciting new fonts
- ▼ Change the margins
- ▼ Add page numbers
- ▼ Change the line spacing
- ▼ Put today's date in a document
- ▼ Put an automatically updating date in a document

ow. What a list of topics. Think of this chapter as a menu. of *for matting changes*. (This chapter contains the chef's selections.) Browse through the formatting changes you can make and pick and choose what works for you.

Some sections have a lot of steps. Don't let that intimidate you. This chapter is essentially a set of formatting recipes; you can just follow along.

Using Tabs and Indents

To make a document more readable, you can show where one paragraph starts and the next begins. Do this with the Tab key. To call attention to a particular paragraph, use the Indent feature.

Tabbing

Whenever you want the first line in a paragraph to start a bit further to the right than the rest of the paragraph, just press Tab. Then type the paragraph. If you've already typed the paragraph, just move the cursor to the beginning of the paragraph and press Tab.

Checklist

▼ If you want the first line indented even more, press Tab twice—or as many times as you want. You can tell how far the text is indented by looking at the **Pos** measurement on the status line.

▼ Don't press Tab at the beginning of each line when you want an indented paragraph. That's what the Indent feature is for.

▼ By default, each time you press Tab, your cursor moves one-half inch. You can change this distance if you want. If you want to know how, read "Changing Your Tab Stops" in Chapter 11.

Indent a Paragraph

It's always impressive to quote an expert when you need to give your opinion some backing:

> Dr. Spock agrees that you should not swing a toddler around by his ankles after he has eaten an entire bag of Iced Animal Cookies.

When a quote is more than three lines long, it belongs in a paragraph of its own. The entire paragraph should be indented, to set it apart from regular text.

To indent a paragraph, move the cursor to where the paragraph will begin. (If you've already typed the paragraph, move the cursor to the beginning of it.) Press F4 to make the whole paragraph jump one-half inch to the right.

TIP

Use the Indent feature to make lists. At the beginning of a line, type a list number and a period, such as **1.** or **2.** Or, if you prefer bullets (•), press Ctrl-2, and then press the asterisk key (*) twice to make a bullet. Next, press F4 to start indenting. Type the text for the list item; then press Enter twice. Repeat these steps for each item in the list. Your numbers or bullets appear in a column to the left of the indented text—just like in the checklists in this book.

▼ If you want to indent further to the right, press F4 more than once. You can get a good idea of where the left side of the paragraph will be by looking at the `Pos` measurement in the status line.

▼ You can indent both the left and right sides of a paragraph. Press Shift-F4 instead of just F4.

For Bibliographies Only

You might want to indent everything but the first line of a paragraph. This is called a *hanging indent* and is useful for bibliographies.

To make a hanging indent, move the cursor to the beginning of the paragraph, press F4 to indent the paragraph, and then press Shift-Tab to move the cursor back to the margin. The first line of your paragraph won't be indented, but every other line in the paragraph will be. Here's how it will look:

> Spock, Dr. "The Dangers of the Swinging Toddlers Who Have Eaten Iced Animal Cookies." *Pediatric Care*, no. 7 (July 1988): 12-63.

TIP

If you want to make the headings in your document stand out from the rest of the text, try this technique. Press Shift-Tab, type the heading, and then press Enter. You might also want to make the text bold and big, which you learn about later in this chapter.

Centering Text

(Stuck in the middle with you)

If you've ever had to center a line of text using a typewriter, you'll be pleased to know that WordPerfect will not make you participate in the same kinds of mathematical gymnastics. In fact, telling WordPerfect to center a title is simple.

Center One Line

To center only one line, move the cursor to the beginning of the line where you want your centered text. This line should be empty. Press Shift-F6. The cursor jumps to the middle of the line. Type the text you want centered. As you type, the line automatically adjusts so that the text stays centered. You can edit the line later and it will *still* stay centered. Pretty amazing. Press Enter to end the centered line.

Checklist

▼ Shift-F6 doesn't work with text that's more than one line long. If you type so much that the cursor wraps to the next line, neither line will be centered.

▼ You can use Shift-F6 to center a line that you've already typed. Move the cursor to the beginning of the line and press Shift-F6. The text jumps a little to the right, becoming centered.

continues

▼ If your text doesn't look perfectly centered in relation to the rest of the text on the screen, don't worry—it's centered properly and it will print centered perfectly. WordPerfect does its best to show centered lines as being centered on-screen, but it doesn't always work as well as you'd hope. If you want to make *sure* that the line is centered, use the View Document feature. (Chapter 6 tells you all about this feature.)

▼ If you want to center large chunks of text (10 or more lines), use *center justification*. This scary-sounding but rather simple, concept is explained in Chapter 11 in the section "Justifying Text."

"I HATE THIS!"

I have to squint to make the text look centered!

The Center feature doesn't center your text between the left and right edges of the page. Instead, WordPerfect centers text between the left and right *margins*. What's the difference? Well, if your left and right margins are the same size (each 1 inch, for example), there's no real difference. If your margins are different, though (say you have a left margin of 3 inches and a right margin of one-half inch), the center between your margins is different than the center between the edges of the page. Your "centered" text won't look centered at all. What does all this mean? If you're going to use Center, you ought to have even-sized margins.

Centering a Bunch of Lines

Sometimes a title has several lines and you want them all centered. Go ahead and type them normally, pressing Enter at the end of each line. Now you can use the Block feature together with Center to make the whole thing centered at once. Move the cursor to the beginning of the first line you want centered, press Alt-F4, and then move the cursor to the end of the last line you want centered. All the lines you want centered should be highlighted now. Press Shift-F6. WordPerfect shows this prompt:

```
[Just:Center]? No (Yes)
```

This prompt is asking you, "Do you want to center the block?" Press Y for Yes. Each line of the block of text jumps to the center of the page.

Aligning Text at the Right Margin

Many business-letter writing styles call for the date at the right margin; a few call also for the return address at the right margin. This section tells you how to right-align text that you type.

Aligning One Line

To align one line at the right margin, move the cursor to a new line. This line is where you want to place the right-aligned text. Next press Alt-F6. The cursor jumps to the right side of the screen, showing you it's ready for you to type the text.

Type the text. Notice that as you type, the cursor stays at the right side of the screen, and text you've already typed moves left. In other words, the thing you last typed is always up against the right margin. Press Enter to go to a new line. The cursor jumps back to the left side of the screen.

Checklist

▼ You can make text that you've already typed align with the right margin. Move the cursor to the beginning of the text you want flush right, and then press Alt-F6. The text jumps to the right side of the page.

▼ The text you type shouldn't be more than one line long. If it is, the second line won't be flush with the right margin.

EXPERTS ONLY

Alignment combo

You some day might want a line that has some text on the left side, some in the center, and some on the right, like this:

This is left   This is center   This is right

You can do this using the Center and Flush Right features together. Move your cursor to a new line; then type the text you want to be the left side of the page. Next, press Shift-F6 for Center, and type the text you want to be in the center. Finally, press Alt-F6 and type the text you want to be on the right. When you finish, press Enter to go to a new line.

Aligning Lots of Lines

You can make several existing lines flush with the right margin. First, you block the lines; then you use the Flush Right feature.

To block the lines, decide what text you want flush right. Then move the cursor to the beginning of the first line of the text, press Alt-F4, and move the cursor to the end of the last line. Next, press Alt-F6. You see this prompt:

[Just:Right]? No (Yes)

WordPerfect is asking you, "Do you want the block of text flush right?" Press Y for Yes.

TIP

If you want to make a large part of your document flush right, don't use the Flush Right feature. Instead, use the Justification feature. Take a look at the section "Justifying Text" in Chapter 11 for more about the Justification feature.

Using Bold, Underline, and Italic

(Adding oomph)

Bold, underline, and italic can help you add special emphasis to important words. Here's how you type a word—either bold, underline, or italic—that stands out from the crowd:

1. Move the cursor to where you want to type the emphasized text.

2. Depending on whether you want bold, underline, or italic, press one of these keystrokes:

▼ Press F6 to make text **bold**

▼ Press F8 to make text <u>underlined</u>

▼ Press Ctrl-F8, A, I to make text *italic*

Look at the measurement next to Pos in the status line. This measurement changes color to show that a text emphasizer is turned on.

3. Type the text you want emphasized.

The text appears, sometimes emphasized the way you chose, other times in a different color. This is because some computers just can't show text emphasis, so they have to fake it by using different colors.

4. Press the right-arrow key to turn off the text emphasizer.

If you used more than one emphasizer (maybe bold and italic), press the right-arrow key once for each emphasizer you used.

Checklist

▼ If you're using bold or underline, the same key that turns the attribute on also turns it off.

▼ You can add emphasis to existing text. First, block the text by moving the cursor to the beginning of the section you want to emphasize, pressing Alt-F4, and then moving the cursor so that it's after the last character you want emphasized. Next, just press the keystrokes shown in step 2.

▼ You might decide to remove the emphasis from text. This is sort of a nuisance to do in WordPerfect, because you have to deal with a strange creature called Reveal Codes. Read "Erase Unwanted Formatting by Using Reveal Codes" in Chapter 12 to learn how to remove attributes you've added to your text.

Giving Your Documents a Font Lift

Let's take a quick walk down memory lane. Back in the old days, when the IBM Selectric typewriter reigned supreme, the part of the machine that actually struck the page was a little metal ball covered with letters and numbers. If you wanted your documents to have a different look, you could remove one ball and stick in a different one. The different balls had the same letters on them, but the letters looked different.

That's the idea behind computer *fonts*. You've always got the same letters and numbers available, but you can give those letters and numbers a different look. In other words, a computer font is just the electronic version of one of those typewriter balls that were so easy to lose.

With a computer, however, it's *really* easy to change the font in your documents. Here are some different fonts:

Times
Helvetica
Palatino
`Courier`

What fonts you have depend on your printer. Different printers let you print different fonts. Experiment with different fonts to see which ones look good where.

Choosing a Font

Here's how you choose a new font:

1. Move the cursor to where you want the new font to begin.

This new font will apply from your cursor to the end of the document, or until you change the font again. If you want the font in effect for the whole document, press Home, Home, up-arrow key to move the cursor to the beginning of the document.

2. Press Ctrl-F8.

This menu appears:

```
1 Size; 2 Appearance; 3 Normal; 4 Base Font;
5 Print Color: 0
```

3. Press F for Base Font.

Don't worry about what the *base* in *Base Font* means. It doesn't matter.

A menu of fonts appears. The menu might only contain two or three fonts—or it might contain dozens. It all depends on your printer.

4. Use arrow keys to highlight the font you want to use; then press Enter.

One of two things happens. Either the menu disappears and you go back to the document screen (in which case you're done), or a prompt appears:

```
Point size:
```

If this prompt appears, you need to type a number—the bigger the number, the bigger the font. Type **12** for normal-size text, **24** for titles, or **36** for really big, half-inch-high titles. You can also type larger or smaller numbers. Press Enter when you've typed the number you want; WordPerfect goes back to the document screen.

BUZZWORDS

POINT

A *point* is a measurement—like inches, but much smaller. There are 72 points per inch.

Pontificating on Fonts

▼ When the Font menu appears, an asterisk is beside the font that's currently in use.

▼ If you are in the Font menu and decide you don't want to select a font after all, press F1 to return to your document screen.

▼ If you want to change the font for only part of a document, move to the beginning of where you want the new font and follow steps 2 through 4. Then move to where you want to return to the original font and follow steps 2 through 4 again, this time selecting the original font.

▼ Some fonts in your Font list may have Bold, Italics, or even Bold Italics as part of the font name. It's not a good idea to select these as your font. Instead, choose the plain version of the font and turn on bold or italic when you need them with the appropriate WordPerfect command keys.

continues

▼ Experiment with mixing fonts before you use them in documents. Some font combinations work well; others can make you dizzy.

▼ The View Document feature doesn't show the exact font you're using. If you want to see how a font looks, you have to print some text in that font.

CAUTION

After you get used to the Font feature, you'll be tempted to use it all over the place. For Pete's sake, fight the temptation. If you use too many fonts in a document, your text will look like one of those anonymous threats people tie to bricks and throw through windows.

Adjusting Your Margins

(Corral your text)

Margins are the white space that surrounds the text on a page. Word-Perfect sets up standard 1-inch margins all the way around the page. These settings work for most documents. If you need to tinker with the number of words on the page—cram more text or less text—change the margins.

Top and Bottom Margins

Here's how you set new top and bottom margins:

1. Press Home, Home, up-arrow key to go to the top of the document.

New margin settings apply from the position of the cursor when you change the margin to the end of the document. Or to the next place you change the margins. You usually want to be at the top of the document when you change margins so that the new settings apply for the entire document.

2. Press Shift-F8 to bring up the Format menu.

3. Press P for Page.

The Format: Page menu appears. Here's where you set the top and bottom margin settings.

4. Press M for Margins.

The cursor jumps over to the Top number. This number, and the number below it, are your current top and bottom margins.

5. Type a measurement for your top margin, press Enter, type a measurement for your bottom margin, and press Enter again.

Use decimals for your measurements. For instance, if you want a 1 1/2-inch margin, type **1.5**. If you want a 3/4-inch margin, type **.75**. You don't have to type the inch marks after the numbers. WordPerfect puts them in for you.

6. Press F7.

CHAPTER 10

TIP

If you want to change only the top or bottom margin, just press Enter when the cursor is positioned at the measurement you don't want to change. That measurement will remain unchanged. This trick works for setting left and right margins, also.

"I HATE THIS!"

But my cursor is on the page! Why isn't the margin changed?

When you set the top and bottom margins, make sure that the cursor is positioned at the *top* of the first page that the margins apply to. If the cursor isn't at the top of the page, your new margin settings won't take effect until the next page.

Left and Right Margins

This is how you change the left and right margins:

1. Press Home, Home, up-arrow key to go to the top of the document.

New margin settings apply from the position of the cursor when you change the margin to the end of the document. Or to the next place you change the margins. You usually want to be at the top of the document when you change margins so that the new settings apply for the entire document.

2. Press Shift-F8 to bring up the Format menu.

3. Press L to move to the Format: Line menu.

4. Press M for Margins.

Your cursor hops, skips, and jumps to the Left measurement. This measurement and the one below it are the current left and right margin settings.

5. Type a measurement for the left margin, press Enter, type a measurement for the right margin, and press Enter again. Don't bother typing the inch marks, WordPerfect takes care of that.

6. Press F7 to return to the document screen.

TIP

Changing margin settings is a good way to increase or decrease the amount of text that fits on a page. If you need more room to fit all your text on a page, make smaller margins—say, $3/4$-inch margins instead of 1-inch margins.

College students take note: If you need a document to take up more pages, make your margins a little bigger. Most college professors can't tell the difference between a 1-inch margin and a $1^1/4$-inch margin. Most college professors can, however, tell the difference between a 1-inch margin and a 2-inch margin, so don't take this little deception to the extreme.

"I HATE THIS!"

No 0-inch margins allowed!

If you're using a laser printer, you can't set margins of 0 inches because laser printers can't print clear out to the edge of the paper. If you try to set margins of 0 inches, WordPerfect will automatically adjust them to your printer's minimum margin capabilities.

Adding Page Numbers

Page numbers are vital for keeping a document in order. Suppose that you copy a 22-page report. Suddenly the copier takes a disliking to the report and spits the pages out in a scrambled order. Without page numbers, all the king's horses and all the king's men won't be able to put the report back together again.

Setting the Page Number

For long documents, add page numbers. Here's how you do it:

1. Press Home, Home, up-arrow key to go to the top of the document.

New margin settings apply from the position of the cursor when you change the margin to the end of the document. Or to the next place you change the margins. You usually want to be at the top of the document when you change margins so that the new settings apply for the entire document.

2. Press Shift-F8 to bring up the Format menu.

3. Press P to bring up the Format: Page menu.

This menu contains all the features that can repeat page after page, like headers, footers, and—of course—page numbering.

4. Press N for Page Numbering.

Now you're in the Format: Page Numbering menu.

5. Press P for Page Number Position.

A menu appears in the form of three boxes. These boxes are supposed to be like pages, and the numbers in the boxes show where in the pages you can have page numbers.

TIP

> For most documents, you can ignore the two boxes on the right. Those are only useful if you're going to have your document bound and printed.

6. Press a number corresponding to the part of the page that will have page numbers. For example, press 3 if you want page numbers in the upper right corner of your pages. Press 6 if you want page numbers in the bottom center.

As soon as you press a number, WordPerfect takes you back to the Format: Page Numbering menu.

7. Press F7 to go back to the document screen.

You're all set, page-numbering-wise. The page numbers aren't visible while you type. You won't see them until you either print your document or use the View Document feature.

Page 2 on Page Numbers

There are lots of things you can do to tinker with the placement of page numbers. Here are some ideas:

▼ You may not want page numbering to begin until the second page—that's the way things usually work in letters and reports. To start page numbering on the second page, move the cursor to page 2 before you assign page numbering.

▼ You can add text next to the page number. For example, the page number could read *Page 3* rather than just *3*. To add text, follow steps 1 through 6 in the basic steps. When you get to step 7, though, press S for Page Number Style. Your cursor will be under a ^B, which disappears when you start typing. Type the text you want to be by the page number, such as **Page**. Press the space bar so that there'll be a space between your text and the page number. Press Enter when you're done; then press F7 to return to your document.

▼ You can make automatic page numbering part of a WordPerfect header or footer. For instructions (as well as an explanation of "headers" and "footers"), see "Creating Headers and Footers" in Chapter 11.

▼ If you want to insert the page number within the text of your document, press Ctrl-B where you need the page number. ^B appears at the cursor. When you print the document, though, WordPerfect sees that ^B and replaces it with the current page number.

▼ If you want automatic page numbering, but need to start at a number different from 1, follow steps 1 through 6; then press N for New Page Number. Type the number you want to start with, and then press Enter. Press F7 to go back to the document.

"I HATE THIS!"

Hey! Where's the page number?

When you turn on page numbering, it inserts an invisible code into your document. If this code isn't the first thing on that page, page numbering won't take effect until the following page. Chapter 12 helps you with decoding the codes.

Changing Line Spacing

You might get tired of single-spacing and want to try a different line spacing (double-space, triple-space). Here's how you do it:

1. Move the cursor to where you want to change line spacing.

If you want to change your line spacing right from the beginning of the document, press Home, Home, up-arrow key. If you want to change line spacing starting with a certain paragraph, move the cursor to the beginning of that paragraph.

2. Press Shift-F8 to display the increasingly familiar Format menu.

3. Press L for Line.

The Format: Line menu appears.

4. Press S for Line Spacing.

Your cursor jumps to the Line Spacing number. (This number is just right of 6 - Line Spacing.)

5. Type the new spacing number and press Enter.

Type numbers like **2** for double spacing and **3** for triple spacing. You can also use decimals, like **1.5**, **2.2**, **1.18**, and so forth.

6. Press F7 to return to the document screen.

Your new line spacing shows up . . . sort of. It shows things like single, double, and triple spacing, but has to round off for things like 1 1/2 spacing.

Checklist

▼ You can have more than one line spacing change in a document. Each line spacing change stays in effect from where you make the change until the end of the document. Or until the next line spacing change.

▼ Line spacing changes can be used to increase or decrease the amount of text that fits on a page. Need more space? Use a smaller Line Spacing number (like .9 instead of 1, or 1.8 instead of 2). Need your text to take up more space? Add an extra tenth to your line spacing.

Putting the Date in Your Document

(Wanna date?)

No need to look at that wall calendar any time you need to put the date in your document. WordPerfect has a feature that plops the date in as

fast as you can press a couple of keys. You can put in today's date, or you can put in a special date code that automatically updates itself every time you retrieve the document.

Insert Today's Date

When you write a letter or report, you usually want to include the current date. That way, if you ever retrieve the document again, you can see when you wrote the letter.

To insert the current date into your document, first move the cursor to where you want the date to appear. Next, press Shift-F5 to bring up the Date menu, which looks like this:

```
1 Date Text; 2 Date Code; 3 Date Format; 4 Outline;
5 Para Num; 6 Define: 0
```

Press T for Date Text to insert the date into your document. It will look like:

April 4, 1993

"I HATE THIS!"

January 1, 1980. Am I in a time warp?

If the wrong date appears, your computer's clock needs to be set. Find someone who's not afraid to brave the dangers of DOS and ask this person to fix your computer's clock. (Computer time is handled by the DOS monster, not by WordPerfect.)

After you've inserted the date using this technique, the date is just normal text. You can edit it or delete it just like you would any other text in your document.

Insert a Date that Automatically Updates

WordPerfect lets you insert a date that is updated every time you open the document. This little feature might come in handy on a report or memo you are writing. You want the date that you *finish* the document to show up, not the date you started it.

When you want an auto-updating date, move the cursor to where the date should go. Press Shift-F5. The Date menu appears. Just press C for Date Code. The date appears (in the April 4, 1993 format). This date will update itself any time you retrieve or print this document.

Checklist

▼ WordPerfect uses the computer's clock to figure out the date. If the wrong date appears, find someone familiar with updating the computer clock to set the proper date for you.

▼ Although this date *looks* like regular text, it's really a special computer code. You can't edit the automatically updating date. If you want to delete it, move your cursor so that it's right after the date; then press Backspace once.

CHAPTER 11

Features You'll Use a Few Times Per Week

IN A NUTSHELL

- ▼ Justify your text
- ▼ Change your tab stops
- ▼ Change the font used for all new documents
- ▼ Put symbols and letters from international alphabets into your documents
- ▼ Center your text between the top and bottom margins
- ▼ Create headers and footers

Fold down a corner on this page. Or stick a Post-It on one of the edges. This chapter covers stuff that you'll need to do every few days—not enough that you should bother memorizing the procedures, but often enough that you'll want to be able to find these pages quickly.

The features included here can make your documents look really polished and professional. For example, you learn how to make your text line up on both margins—like it does in newspapers and magazines. Or make your text centered—for an invitation or poem.

You learn to make the distance between tab stops larger or smaller. You find out how to make your text centered between the top and bottom margins, which is handy when you're making a cover page. You create a *header*, which is a line or two of text you want to be at the top of the page. (By the way, a *footer* is the same thing, only it shows up at the bottom of the page.) All this, and we'll even throw in a free Ginsu knife.

Justifying Text

(Text to the left, text to the right)

Different types of documents need to have different "looks." A letter to an old high school chum should have a different look than an official memo to your employees. A party invitation should have a different look than a company report. Using different *line justification* is a good way to give your document a look that matches its message. (If you're fuzzy about line justification, check out the figure in this section.)

BUZZWORDS

JUSTIFICATION

Justification describes how words line up with the left and right margins. If you have left justification, words line up at the left margin, but not at the right. Right justification has words line up at the right margin, but not at the left. Center justification centers lines between the two margins, and full justification has text lined up on both the left and right margins, the way they do in newspapers and some magazines.

Examples of how each type of justification looks.

Left-justified text:	**Right-justified text:**
Dear Elden , You may already be a winner. Yes, you have been selected as one of the finalists in the Hocus-Pocus Sweepstakes.	Betty McDaniel 1300 South Street Augatuck, MI 60788 (212) 555-6011
Center-justified text:	**Full-justified text:**
You are hereby invited to The Nelsons' Second Annual Clam-Bake	**Tabloid Journalists Kill Elvis!** Four tabloid journalists were apprehended today for the murder of Elvis Presley. Apparently, the King really was alive and had recently announced his intentions of coming out of hiding.

Making the Change

When you use this feature, the justification is in effect from your cursor position to the end of the document. Or until you make another justification change—whichever comes first.

CHAPTER 11

This is how you change your text's justification:

1. Move the cursor to the beginning of the line where you want the new justification.

You can set the justification and then type the text, or set the justification in front of text that already exists. If you want the justification to take effect at the very beginning of the document, press Home, Home, up-arrow key; this moves the cursor to the beginning of the document.

2. Press Shift-F8 to bring up the Format menu.

3. Press L for Line.

4. Press J for Justification.

This prompt appears:

```
Justification: 1 Left; 2 Center; 3 Right; 4 Full: 0
```

5. Press the letter for the type of justification you want. Press L for Left, C for Center, R for Right, or F for Full.

6. Press F7 to return to the document screen.

All the text from the cursor to the end of the document now appears in the new justification.

Justifying justification

▼ You can have more than one justification setting in a document. For example, you might want to have part of a document center-justified, and the rest left-justified. To apply different justifications at different parts of the document, just follow the steps at each point you want a justification change.

▼ WordPerfect's default justification is Full. If your document is going to have full justification throughout, you don't need to do anything.

▼ Don't use this technique to change the justification for just a line or two. There's a much easier way, which you learn about in Chapter 10.

▼ The steps described here don't work on blocks of text. Chapter 10 tells you how to change the justification on a block of text.

▼ If you want to use left justification all the time, see the next chapter where this trick is showcased.

TIP

If you type columns of numbers in your text and those numbers use decimal places, you can use a feature to align the decimal points like this:

        12.55
        101.77
        2.99

Rather than press Tab, press Ctrl-F6. You see a prompt that says `Align Char = ` . This means the text will be aligned on the period key, which is what you want. Type the number and press Enter. Do the same for the next number.

Changing Your Tab Stops

If you aren't particular about where tabbed text lines up, use the default tab settings (a tab stop every half inch). If you want the text indented more than one-half inch, press Tab again to move over another half inch. Keep pressing Tab until the text is indented as far as you want it.

If you *are* picky about the place the tabs line up and you *don't* like extraneous tabs in the text (you want a tab at 2.8 inches and you want one—and only one—tab stop), you can change the tab settings. (Groups of tab stops are called *tab settings*.)

You can have several different tab settings in a document, and each setting applies until you change tab settings again or until the end of the document—whichever comes first.

Making the Switch

Here's how to set a new tab setting:

1. Move the cursor to the beginning of the line where you want the new tab setting to begin.

If you want the tab setting to be in effect for the whole document, press Home, Home, up-arrow key to move the cursor to the beginning of the document.

2. Press Shift-F8 to bring up the Format menu.

3. Press L for Line.

The Format: Line menu appears.

4. Press T for Tab Set.

The menacing tab stop thing appears at the bottom of your screen, with your document at the top part of the screen.

```
        "What you're trying to say," my wife said, "is that your new
computer has allowed you to make a quantum leap in the quality of
your puttering."
        "But I never have to wait for the machine to make
calculations. My print jobs print pronto. My cursor moves at the
speed of light. That counts for something, doesn't it?"  I sure
hoped it did.
        "For the sake of argument, we'll assume for the moment that it
does count for something.  Let's figure out just exactly how much."
Somehow, the way she said that made me less than enthused to find
L.....L.....L.....L.....L.....L.....L.....L.....L.....L.....L.....L.
!     ^     ^     ^     ^     ^     ^     ^     ^     ^     ^     !
0"         +1"        +2"        +3"        +4"        +5"        +6"
Ctrl-End (clear tabs); Enter Number (set tab); Del (clear tab);
Type; Left; Center; Right; Decimal; .= Dot Leader; Press Exit when done.
```

The tab ruler —

5. Make any changes to your tab setting; then press F7 twice to return to the document screen.

Checklist

▼ The row with dots and L's on it is your actual tab setting. Each L stands for a left-justified tab stop. The row with the numbers tells you where those tab stops are set. This strip of dots and L's is called your *tab ruler*.

▼ The numbers (such as 0", +1", +2", and so forth) stand for the distance from the left margin. If you have a 1-inch left margin, the 1-inch tab would be 2 inches from the left side of the page, because the 1-inch left margin *plus* 1 inch from the left margin is 2 inches, total.

continues

▼ You can use the left- and right-arrow keys to move the cursor along the tab ruler.

▼ To remove a tab, move the cursor under the tab and press Delete.

▼ To create a new tab, move the cursor to where you want the tab and press L.

▼ Press Ctrl-End to remove all the tabs from the cursor to the end of the ruler.

▼ To put a tab stop at a certain position on the page, just type that position and press Enter. For example, if you want a tab stop 3.7 inches from the left margin, type **3.7**, and then press Enter. A new tab stop appears where you specified.

▼ To put tab stops at regular intervals on the tab ruler, type the first place you want a tab stop, press a comma, and then type the distance that should be between each tab stop. Suppose, for example, that you want tab stops every quarter inch (0.25") and want the first one to begin right at the left margin (0"). Just type **0",0.25"** and press Enter. (It's really easy once you get used to how WordPerfect thinks.)

TIP

You can drag an existing tab stop to another position. Use the arrow keys to move the cursor under the tab stop you want to move. Then hold down the Ctrl key while you press the left- or right-arrow key to move the tab to its new position. As you move the tab stops, the text above the ruler moves too so that you can see how the text will look with the new setting. Note, however, that you cannot move a tab past an existing tab.

Using Fancy Tab Stops

All those L's on the tab ruler stand for *left tabs*. Left tabs are the most common type of tabs. You can set several other tabs. You put other tabs on the tab ruler by moving the cursor to where you want the tab stop, and then pressing the letter for the type of tab you want. You can set these types of tabs:

Tab name	Important stuff about the tab
Left	This is the normal type of tab. Press L to set a left tab. When you tab to a left tab stop, text that comes after the tab flows to the right.
Center	Press C to set a center tab. When you tab to a center tab stop, the text you type is centered over that tab—not centered between the margins. Use this type of tab for column headings.
Right	Press R to set a right tab. When you tab to a right tab stop, the text you type flows to the left, which means that the *end* of your text is at the tab stop. Use this type of tab for headings that appear above columns of numbers.
Decimal	Press D to set a decimal tab. Use this type of tab when you need to type a column of numbers with decimals. All of your numbers will line up on the decimal point, making things easier to add.
Dot Leader	This type of tab stop can be used with any of the other types. After you've created a left, center, right, or decimal tab, press a period to make the tab a dot leader tab, as well. By doing this, a row of dots appears from your previous position to the beginning of the tab, like this: Recipes for Success 123

Changing the Default Font

(Hooked on fonts)

When you don't specify a font, WordPerfect picks one for you—generally a typewriter-like concoction that may or may not be to your liking. This font is called the *default*. Fortunately, you can specify a different default font.

To change the font WordPerfect uses for all new documents, follow these steps:

1. Press Shift-F7.

The Print menu appears.

2. Press S for Select Printer.

The default font is part of the way your printer works, so it's included in the Printer part of the program.

The Print: Select Printer menu appears. The printer you use should be highlighted and have an asterisk (*) next to it.

3. Press E to edit your printer definition.

Don't worry. That sounds a lot more difficult than it is. You're just going to be selecting a font—you don't need to run for a screwdriver or anything.

The Select Printer: Edit menu appears.

4. Press F for Initial Base Font.

A font list appears, just like in the Font menu you get when you press Ctrl-F8, 4.

5. Use arrow keys to highlight the font you want to use; then press Enter.

If the `Point size` prompt appears at the bottom of the screen, you need to type a number—the bigger the number, the bigger the font. (Try typing **10** or **12** to start.) After you type the number, press Enter.

6. Press F7 three times to go back to your document screen.

Now when you create a document and don't specify a certain font, WordPerfect will automatically use the font you just selected. You aren't locked into this font, however; you can still choose other fonts when you need them. (Flip back to Chapter 10 for the dirt on changing fonts.)

Putting Interesting Characters into Your Documents

(What a character!)

If you occasionally need to type a word or phrase in a foreign language, you'll also need to be able to put those accent marks and squiggly things over certain letters. You may even need to make an upside-down question mark (¿) or exclamation point (¡).

If you pretty much stick to English in your documents, you may still want to know how to put a • character (for making lists) or a happy face (to show people what a cheerful person you are) into your document. WordPerfect lets you add all these funky characters *really* easily.

First, press Ctrl-2; then type certain characters or numbers. It's that easy.

TIP

Note that you press Ctrl-2, not Ctrl-F2. And you won't see anything until you finish pressing the series of characters.

This chart shows you how to create some basic characters:

To make this character	Press Ctrl-2, then press . .
Anything with an accent over it, like á, é, í	The letter, followed by an apostrophe, like **a'**
Anything with a tilde over it, like ñ	The letter, followed by a tilde, like **n~**
Anything with umlauts, like ä, ö, ü	The letter, followed by quote marks, like **a"**
ç, Ç	**c,** **C,**
æ Æ	**ae** **AE**
¡	**!!**
¿	**??**
¼	**/4**
½	**/2**
©	**co**
™	**tm**
®	**ro**
■	******
¢	**c/**
—	**--** (this makes an em-dash which is good for separating phrases)
–	**n-** (this makes an en-dash, which is used to separate parts of phone numbers)
☺	**5,7** then **Enter**
☹	**5,26** then **Enter**
⊠	**5,25** then **Enter**
£	**4,11** then **Enter**
¥	**4,12** then **Enter**
§	**4,6** then **Enter**
♪	**5,9** then **Enter**

Some of these characters just appear as boxes on the document screen. Not to worry; they'll print fine.

Centering a Page between Top and Bottom Margins

When you make a cover page for a report, you usually want the text centered between your top and bottom margins. To center everything on a page between the top and bottom margins, follow these instructions:

1. Move the cursor to the *top* of the page you want centered between the top and bottom margins. If you have the cursor anywhere but at the top of the page, the page won't be centered.

You can move your cursor to the top of the current page by pressing Ctrl-Home, up-arrow key.

2. Press Shift-F8.

The Format menu appears.

3. Press P for Page.

4. Press C for Center Page.

5. Press Y for Yes.

6. Press F7 to return to the document screen.

From the document screen, it won't look like the page is centered between the top and bottom margins. Don't worry; it is. If you don't trust

WordPerfect, you can preview the document (which is explained in Chapter 6).

Checklist

▼ These steps only make the *current* page centered between the top to bottom margins. If you want to center another page, go to the top of that page and follow these steps again.

▼ These steps center the page between the top and bottom. If you also want to center between the left and right margins, go back to the section "Justifying Text" at the beginning of this chapter. That section teaches you about center justification (centering between the left and right margins).

Creating Headers and Footers

A *header* is text that shows up at the top of every page in a document. A *footer* is the same kind of thing, but it shows up at the bottom of the page rather than the top. The main purpose of headers and footers is to give your documents continuity. You might, for example, include your company name or the title of your report in the header. The footer might include the date or page number.

Headers (Heads Up)

Here's how to put a header into your document:

1. Move the cursor to the top of the first page that you want to have the header.

If you want the header to start on the first page, press Home, Home, up-arrow key.

2. Press Shift-F8 to open the Format menu.

3. Press P for Page.

4. Press H to create a header.

This prompt appears at the bottom of the screen:

```
1 Header A; 2 Header B: 0
```

5. Press A for Header A.

Another menu appears at the bottom of the screen:

```
1 Discontinue; 2 Every Page; 3 Odd Pages;
4 Even Pages; 5 Edit: 0
```

6. Press P to have the header appear on every page.

An editing screen appears that looks a lot like the regular document screen.

7. Type the header text.

The title of your document, the date it was created, your name, and a page number code are common things to put in a header.

8. When you're done creating the header, press F7 twice to return to the document screen.

You won't be able to see the header while you're writing your document. You need to print the document or use View Document to see the header.

Footers

You do just about the same thing to create a footer:

1. Move the cursor to the top of the first page that you want to have the footer.

If you want the footer to start at the first page, press Home, Home, up-arrow key.

2. Press Shift-F8 to start the Format menu.

3. Press P for Page.

4. Press F to create a footer.

This prompt appears at the bottom of the screen:

```
1 Footer A; 2 Footer B: 0
```

5. Press A for Footer A.

Another menu appears at the bottom of the screen:

```
1 Discontinue; 2 Every Page; 3 Odd Pages;
4 Even Pages; 5 Edit: 0
```

6. Press P to have the footer appear on every page.

An editing screen appears that looks pretty much like your regular document screen.

7. Type the footer text.

The title of your document, the date it was created, your name, and a page number code are common things to put in a footer.

8. When you're finished creating the footer, press F7 twice to return to your document screen.

You won't be able to see the footer while you're writing the document. You need to print the document or use View Document to see the footer.

Header and footer ideas

▼ If you want the current page number in your header or footer, move your cursor to where you want the page number and press Ctrl-B. This puts a ^B code into your document. When you print the document, WordPerfect replaces the code with the correct page number.

▼ You can have the current date as part of the header or footer. Just press Shift-F5, C to insert the date. This date updates automatically whenever you retrieve or print the document.

▼ If you decide you want to make changes to a header or footer you've already created, follow the same steps, except in step 6, press E instead of P. This takes you into the editing screen where you created the header or footer. Make the changes you need, and then press F7 twice to return to the document screen.

▼ If you don't want a header or footer to appear on the first page of a document, move the cursor a couple of lines down in the document before you create the header or footer. The header or footer will start on the second page.

▼ You can have both headers and footers on each page in your document. You're not restricted to having one or the other.

CHAPTER 12

Formatting Features You'll Rarely Use
(But Are Still Nice to Know)

IN A NUTSHELL

▼ Make your text larger or smaller

▼ Make sure certain parts of your document stay together on the same page

▼ Change the default justification

▼ Put footnotes and endnotes into your documents

▼ Clean up your document with the Reveal Codes feature

There are a good handful of features that you need to use all the time in WordPerfect, and dozens of features that you may never need to use at all. The features in this chapter fall somewhere in between. You probably won't often need them, but when you do, you'll be glad WordPerfect includes them.

Make Your Text Larger or Smaller

There are certain parts of your documents that need to stand out. For example, you want your titles and section headings to reach out of the paper, grab your reader by the lapels, and scream "Look at me!" The way that most books (including this one) showcase titles and headings is by making them bigger. WordPerfect has a way of achieving this effect.

If you are a lawyer and like plenty of small print, or if you are writing to Munchkins, you can use these same steps to make the text small.

This is how you tell WordPerfect what size to make the text you are about to type:

1. Move the cursor to where you want to type the different-sized text.

2. Press Ctrl-F8.

Ctrl-F8 is the Font key. You use it to make most of the changes to your text's appearance.

This menu appears:

```
1 Size; 2 Appearance; 3 Normal; 4 Base Font;
5 Print Color: 0
```

3. Press S for Size.

A menu of different size options appears:

```
1 Suprscpt; 2 Subscpt; 3 Fine; 4 Small; 5 Large;
6 Vry Large; 7 Ext Large: 0
```

The sizes listed are all relative to how big your text is in the first place. The size of the text is set by the default font. Flip back to Chapter 11 if you want to learn more about setting the default font.

4. Press one of the numbers, depending on how large you want your text.

For document titles, use V for Very Large or E for Extremely Large. For section headings, L for Large is about right. If you're writing a contract and need some teeny print, press F for Fine.

TIP

> Superscript and Subscript are both the same size as Fine, but 1 Superscript is higher than usual and 2 Subscript is lower than usual. Both of these settings are good for mathematical equations.

5. Type the text.

WordPerfect can't show the text in the different size, but it will show it in a different color or shading to signal you that something about this text is different.

6. Press Ctrl-F8, N to return to normal-sized text.

▼ WordPerfect's ability to change sizes of text depends on your printer. If your printer doesn't have different sizes of text available, WordPerfect can't print the different size. Experiment with typing and printing different sizes before you try them in an important document.

▼ If you want to change the different-sized text back to normal-sized text, move the cursor under the first character that's the different size and press Ctrl-F8, N.

▼ You can change existing text to a different size. Move the cursor to the beginning of the text you want to change, press Alt-F4, and move the cursor past the end of the text. Then follow steps 2 through 4.

Keep Text on the Same Page

(All together now)

Once in a while you'll have a pair of paragraphs that you want together on the same page—no matter what. Or you might have a list as part of your document and want to make sure that the items don't get split between pages. Here's what you do:

1. Move your cursor to the beginning of the section that you don't want split.

2. Press Alt-F4 to turn on Block.

Block On appears in the lower left corner of the screen.

CHAPTER 12

3. Move the cursor past the end of the section you want to keep together.

The section you want to keep from being divided should be highlighted.

4. Press Shift-F8.

This prompt appears:

```
Protect block? No (Yes)
```

5. Press Y for Yes.

The block disappears.

If WordPerfect would usually have put a page break somewhere in the middle of the area you blocked, the page break now comes before the block so that the section isn't split between pages.

Setting the Default Justification

By default, WordPerfect makes your text line up along both the left and right margin by putting extra space between words and letters. If you would rather have left justification (words align on the left margin but not on the right margin), you can make it the default. Text that is left justified is generally easier to read than text that is both left and right justified.

Here's what you do:

1. Press Shift-F1 to bring up the Setup menu.

2. Press I for Initial Settings.

The Setup: Initial Settings menu comes up.

3. Press C for Initial Codes.

A screen similar to the document screen appears. This screen is where you turn on features so that they'll be on every time you start a new document.

4. Press Shift-F8 to bring up the Format menu.

5. Press L for Line to make the Format: Line menu appear.

6. Press J for Justification.

This prompt appears:

```
Justification: 1 Left; 2 Center; 3 Right; 4 Full: 0
```

7. Press L for Left justification.

8. Press F7 three times to get back to the document screen.

Any new documents you create now will be left-justified until you say otherwise. Any documents that you created before you changed the default, however, won't automatically be left-justified when you retrieve them.

Checklist

▼ You can use the Initial Codes to make other changes to the default formatting options. Just follow steps 1 through 3, and then change any settings you want.

▼ For information on other justification changes, take a look at Chapter 11.

Using Footnotes and Endnotes

Footnotes and endnotes are those superscripted numbers (like this[1]) with corresponding messages later in the document. You usually see footnotes in academic papers.

What's the difference between footnotes and endnotes? *Footnote* messages are located at the bottom of the same page as the numbers that refer to them—at the *foot* of the page. *Endnotes*, on the other hand, are all collected at the *end* of the document.

Here are the steps for putting endnotes or footnotes into your documents:

1. Move the cursor to where you want the footnote or endnote reference.

The footnote or endnote *reference* is the little number that goes into your document. The footnote or endnote itself is the message at the bottom of the page or document.

2. Press Ctrl-F7.

This menu appears:

```
1 Footnote; 2 Endnote; 3 Endnote Placement: 0
```

You can create either a footnote or an endnote.

TIP

Don't mix footnotes and endnotes in a single document. Pick one format or the other and stick with it.

---

[1]This is what a footnote looks like, just in case you're curious.

3. Press F to create a footnote, or E to create an endnote.

Up comes another menu:

```
Endnote: 1 Create; 2 Edit; 3 New Number;
4 Options: 0
```

If you pressed F, the same menu appears, although the first word will be "Footnote" instead of "Endnote."

4. Press C to create the note.

An editing screen appears, looking a lot like the one you use to type your documents. There are a couple of differences, though. The bottom left of the editing screen tells you which kind of note you're creating, and the number of your note appears in the upper left corner.

CAUTION

> Don't erase this number! If you do, when you print the document, your note won't have a number beside it.

5. Type the note.

6. Press F7 to return to the document screen.

The footnote number appears just left of the cursor. The number is superscripted (raised a little higher than the other text), but it probably doesn't look superscripted on-screen.

Notes on footnotes

▼ You won't be able to see your footnotes or endnotes in the normal document screen. If you want to see that they're really there, use the View Document feature (explained in Chapter 6) or print the document.

CHAPTER 12

▼ WordPerfect automatically numbers and organizes your footnotes and endnotes. If you suddenly remember you need to put a note between two you've already created, just follow the ordinary steps. WordPerfect puts your note in the right place and renumbers the other notes.

▼ If you need to edit a footnote or endnote, follow steps 1 through 3, and then press E for edit. A prompt appears, asking for the note you want to edit. Type the number and press Enter. You're taken to the editing screen, where you can fix your note. When you're finished, press F7 to go back to the document screen.

▼ If you want to erase a footnote or endnote, move the cursor so that it's under the reference number in your document. Press Delete. If the Reveal Codes window is closed (more on that in a minute), a prompt appears. Press Y to erase the note. WordPerfect renumbers the other notes in the document for you.

▼ The reference numbers to both endnotes and footnotes are superscripted. The corresponding numbers in footnotes are also superscripted, but the corresponding numbers in endnotes aren't— they're normal-sized numbers with a period.

Erase Unwanted Formatting by Using Reveal Codes

(Document housekeeping)

Reveal Codes. What an ominous term—well-named because it is ominous.

169

When you make formatting changes—make words bold or italic, change margins, add headers and footers—WordPerfect is putting codes into your document.

These codes are notes WordPerfect makes to itself: "Start bold here and end it here. Put a header here. Change the margins here." Usually you can't see these codes; they'd just get in the way of your work. When you turn on Reveal Codes, though, you can see all the codes that have been inserted into your document.

Why Look at the Dark World of Reveal Codes?

When would you want to see your codes? When you want to get rid of one, mainly. Some formatting features are hard to remove from your document unless you can see the code that creates it. In that case, you have to travel into the dark world of Reveal Codes.

Turning on Reveal Codes (Brace yourself!)

To turn on Reveal Codes, press Alt-F3.

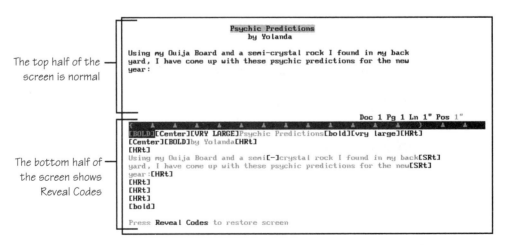

The top half of the screen is normal

The bottom half of the screen shows Reveal Codes

When you turn on Reveal Codes (Alt-F3), a bar splits the screen in two. The top half of the screen is the normal document screen that you're used to. The bottom half of the screen is the Reveal Codes area, and it contains oodles of different-colored text in brackets.

The text in the bottom half of the screen is the same as in the top half of the screen, but it contains all the formatting codes. The different-colored text surrounded by brackets, like [HRt] and [SRt], is the code.

Checklist

▼ You can turn off Reveal Codes at any time by pressing Alt-F3. You can't use F7 or F1 to leave Reveal Codes.

▼ You can do anything within the Reveal Codes window that you can do on the document screen. For example, you can type, erase, and move around. But it's a nuisance because you have to dodge all the codes, so why bother?

▼ If you have an F11 key, you can turn Reveal Codes on and off by pressing that key instead of Alt-F3.

Moving around in the Underworld

When you've got Reveal Codes on, you suddenly have two cursors. When you use your arrow keys, your normal cursor moves around in the top half of the screen. Meanwhile, a matching rectangular cursor moves around in Reveal Codes. This rectangle shows you where you are in Reveal Codes and highlights whatever character or code it's positioned on.

When you move the lower cursor to a code, the code expands and the cursor doesn't move in the top screen.

The Popular [HRt] and [SRt] Codes

More than any other code, you'll see a lot of [HRt] and [SRt] codes in the Reveal Codes screen. [HRt] is the code for *hard return*. WordPerfect puts one of these in your document whenever you press Enter.

[SRt] is WordPerfect's code for a *soft return*—the end of a line. Whenever you're typing and your cursor jumps down to the next line, WordPerfect puts one of these [SRt] codes at the end of the line you just finished.

CAUTION

Don't try to delete [SRt] codes; WordPerfect put them there for a good reason. If you highlight an [SRt] code and press Delete, it's like deleting the space between two words. The words on the left and right of the [SRt] you deleted will be joined.

Housecleaning with Reveal Codes

The main reason you'll use Reveal Codes is to get rid of some formatting change that you just don't want in your document. For example, you might want to get rid of a line spacing change. To do this, you need to find the line spacing code.

Move your cursor to the area of the problem code. Turn on Reveal Codes (press Alt-F3). Move the cursor so that it's on the code you want to erase. Press Delete. The code disappears, and the formatting it makes goes away too. Turn off Reveal Codes by pressing Alt-F3 again.

Many of the codes in WordPerfect are called *paired codes*. These codes come in twos. The first of these two codes turns on a feature, the second turns off the feature. For example, the Bold feature uses paired codes.

Before any bold text, you see [BOLD]. At the end of the bold text is the second of the paired code set: [bold]. When you delete either of the paired codes, the other disappears also.

EXPERTS ONLY

Stripping all codes from a document

You can use the Replace feature to strip all of a certain type of formatting from your document. For example, you can remove all the bold. Or all the tabs. Or all the margin changes. Or all the line spacing changes. Or any other type of code that you want to strip.

Move your cursor to the point where you want to begin removing the formatting. Press Alt-F2. At the w/Confirm? prompt, press Y if you want WordPerfect to ask you at each instance whether to remove formatting; otherwise press N; the -> Srch: prompt is displayed. Press the keys necessary to insert the formatting code you want to remove. To do this, press the same keystrokes you did to put that formatting into your document. For example, if you want to strip underlining from your document, press F8. The [UND] code appears after the Srch prompt.

If the formatting change involves menu choices, press the same keys you use to turn on the feature. (You won't see the full menu, but you will see a one-line menu at the bottom of the screen.)

After you enter the code, press F2 twice.

If you didn't ask to confirm the changes, WordPerfect strips all the formatting that you specified. Otherwise, you need to confirm each change.

Reveal Codes Revealed

Here are some of the most common Reveal Codes:

What the code looks like	What the code means
[HRt]	Hard Return. You pressed Enter.
[SRt]	Soft Return. WordPerfect is wrapping the line.
[HPg]	Hard Page. You pressed Ctrl-Enter to end the page.
[SPg]	Soft Page. WordPerfect ends the page. Don't erase this!
[Tab]	Text moves in one tab stop here.
[→ Indent]	Paragraph is indented on tab stop.
[→ Indent ←]	Left and right ends of paragraph are indented on tab stop.
[← Mar Rel]	Text moves back one tab stop.
[UND][und]	Underline paired codes that mark the beginning and end of <u>underlined</u> text.
[BOLD][bold]	Bold paired codes that mark the beginning and end of **bold** text.
[ITALC][italc]	Italic paired codes that mark the beginning and end of *italic* text.

What the code looks like	What the code means
[FINE][fine]	Fine text size paired codes that mark the beginning and end of very small text.
[SMALL][small]	Small text size paired codes that mark the beginning and end of small text.
[LARGE][large]	Large paired codes that mark the beginning and end of large text.
[VRY LARGE][vry large]	Very Large text size paired codes that mark the beginning and end of very large text.
[EXT LARGE][ext large]	Extra Large text size paired codes that mark the beginning and end of extra large text.
[Center]	A centered line begins.
[Flsh Rgt]	A line begins here that is flush with the right margin.
[Just:Right]	All text is flush with the right margin until further notice.
[Just:Full]	All text is flush against both margins until further notice.
[Just:Center]	All text is centered between left and right margin until further notice.

continues

What the code looks like	What the code means
[Just:Left]	All text is flush with left margin—but not the right margin—until further notice.
[L/R Mar:1.5",1.5"]	New left/right margins go into effect here. The numbers are the new margins.
[T/B Mar:1.5",1.5"]	New top/bottom margins go into effect here. The numbers are the new margins.
[Tab Set:Rel; -1" (big string of numbers here)]	New tab set goes into effect here. The numbers are the tab stop locations and are almost impossible to decipher.
[Center Pg]	Page is centered between top to bottom margins.
[Header A:Every page; (First part of first line of the header goes here)]	Header A begins here. (A similar code is also available for footers.)
[Pg Numbering:Top Right]	Page numbering goes into effect.
[Font:Times 12pt]	Indicated font starts.

PART IV

Handling Files

Includes:

CHAPTER 13

More on Printing
(Forget about the Paperless Office)

IN A NUTSHELL

▼ Get your printer ready

▼ Preview your document

▼ Print the whole document

▼ What to do when the
document won't print

▼ Print some pages but
skip others

▼ Print just one page

▼ Print just a block of text

▼ Print several copies of
your document

▼ Stop a document from
being printed

▼ Set up (install) your
printer

The main reason that most of us use WordPerfect is to make the process of getting words onto paper a little easier. This chapter shows you how to deal with that all-important step in using WordPerfect: printing your documents.

Is Your Printer Ready to Print?

From your viewpoint, printing with a typewriter might seem infinitely easier than printing with a computer. With a typewriter, you punch a key, you get a character. But things *will* be easier with a computer after you print that first document and figure out how to set up everything. (Say this with your fingers crossed.)

The first step is to install your printer. With a little luck, your printer is already installed. If not, flip to the last section in this chapter, "Setting Up a Printer." The next step in the printing process is to get your printer ready:

▼ Make sure that the printer is turned on and is on-line. (To put a printer on-line, press the On Line button on the printer's panel so that the On Line light is lit. Your printer will probably be on-line when you turn it on.)

▼ Make sure that the printer has paper in it. If you have a laser printer (these printers look like a copy machine), just put paper in the tray and slide the tray into the printer. If you have a dot-matrix printer (these printers look like a big fancy typewriter), you'll have to loop and weave and wind the paper through its proper contortions. Get help from someone in the know.

How Will My Document Look on Paper?

(Sneak preview)

When you're typing in WordPerfect, you only have a vague idea of how your text is going to look on the printed page. WordPerfect doesn't show your text actual size. Or your page numbers. Or your margins and graphics. All you see is the text you type—and that's not a lot to go on.

Before you print, you can take a sneak preview of the document by using the View Document feature. It shows you an on-screen picture of how your document will look when printed, including margins, graphics, and other knick-knacks you may have added.

To preview your document, make sure that the document you want to preview is on-screen. (Chapter 4 is the place to go if you don't know how to get a document on-screen.)

If there's a certain page you want to look at first, move the cursor somewhere on that page. Press Shift-F7 to bring up the Print menu, and then press V to choose View Document.

The View Document screen appears, showing a page from your document. Be patient. It may take a moment or two to come up on-screen.

Press F7 when you finish looking at View Document.

Checklist

▼ Move from page to page by pressing Page Up (to go to the previous page) or Page Down (to go to the next page).

continues

▼ If you want to see the document at actual size, press 1 for 100%. If you want to see it *really* big, press 2 for 200%. At these sizes, you won't be able to see the whole page at one time. You can look at different parts of the page by pressing Home, arrow key. (Press the arrow key that points in the direction that you want to look.)

▼ When you want to see the whole page at once, press 3. You can see facing pages by pressing 4.

▼ Jump to any page in the document by pressing Ctrl-Home, typing the page number you want, and pressing Enter.

▼ If everything looks good in View Document, press F7 to return to the editing screen. Or you can go ahead and print the document. Press F1 to go back to the Print menu; then press F for Full document.

Press Shift-F7, V to preview your document.

```
                                                        Report 1
(Music)

Narr:   The story of Little Blue Riding Hood is true. Only the colors have
        been changed, to prevent an investigation.

(Music)

Wolf:   This is the woods. My name is Wednesday. I work out on
        homicide. Monday, February 23. 10:22 a.m. I banged into
        Obidian. Listen . . . told me the sky was falling. I handed her on a
        614 and turned her into the psychiatrist.

        Then a call came in on a 915. While I was on my way to the 915, I
        got a call on a 616. I called up the 616, the 915, and the 616 got
        1755. I handed in my paper to the chief. He corrected it, gave me a
        100 percent, patted me on the head. Told me I was a good cop.

(Music)

        11:45 a.m. It happened. I saw a little girl in a blue hood, walking
        down the path. Bagged in question her.

        —Pardon me ma'am, could I talk to you for a few minutes, ma'am?

Hood:   What about?

Wolf:   Nothing much ma'am. Just want to ask you a few questions,
        ma'am. What's your name?

Hood:   Little Blue Riding Hood.

Wolf:   Yes, ma'am. And where are you going, ma'am?

Hood:   Grandma's house.

Wolf:   Yes, ma'am. And what have you got in your basket, ma'am?
```

`1 100%  2 200%  3 Full Page  4 Facing Pages: 3                    Doc 1 Pg 1`

Printing the Whole Thing

To print, make sure that your printer is ready to go and has enough paper to print the document. Then press Shift-F7. The Print menu appears. Press F for Full Document.

WordPerfect goes back to the document screen, and you can go back to work. Meanwhile, your document starts printing.

Checklist

▼ Don't exit WordPerfect while a document is still printing. If you do, WordPerfect asks whether you want to cancel all print jobs. Press N and wait until WordPerfect finishes printing. Then you can exit.

▼ If you want to print several documents at once, check out Chapter 14, which tells you how to accomplish this feat.

▼ WordPerfect stops printing any time you're in View Document. So, if you've got a document you need printed right away, stay out of the View Document feature until the job is completely printed.

My Printer Won't Print Right!

(Or it won't print at all)

You're finished with that report. What a relief. Now you can print it, mail it, and take off for an early weekend. You send the document to the printer and...nothing. Or maybe something comes out, but it's horribly

mangled. What do you do when things go wrong with your printer? Try the suggestions in this section. If you still can't get things going, find someone who knows about computers and beg him to help you. You can also call WordPerfect Customer Support at 800/541-5170 if you have a laser printer, or 800/541-5160 if you have any other kind of printer.

You Can Print, but It Looks All Wrong

If the awful mess that comes out of your printer bears little or no resemblance to the document you just typed, any of several things could be wrong. This section tells you how to fix the problem.

If the letters print on top of each other or are crammed too close together, one of three things has probably happened:

▼ You're using a laser printer that uses font cartridges and someone took out the font cartridge that you need. Find somebody who understands your printer and ask him to put the cartridge you need back into the printer.

▼ Your printer might be using something called *soft fonts* and they're not loaded. Find the person who knows the most about the printer and ask him whether the fonts have been loaded.

▼ Your copy of WordPerfect might usually use a special program that makes your documents print nicer, but that program isn't working right now. You can try to correct this problem by saving your document, leaving WordPerfect, turning your computer off and then back on, coming back into WordPerfect the way you usually do, and trying to print again.

If strange symbols and characters print in your document or the printer spits out page after page with only a couple of lines on each piece of paper, you've probably got the wrong printer driver selected.

To check which printer driver is selected, press Shift-F7 to bring up the Print menu. Look at the name of the printer to the right of S - Select Printer (six lines from the bottom).

If the name of the printer in this menu doesn't match the name of your printer, press S for Select Printer. A list of printers appears, and your printer should be one of them. (If it isn't, find someone who *really* knows WordPerfect and ask him to help you "install a printer driver.") Use the arrow keys to highlight your printer. Press S for Select, and then F7 to return to your document screen. Try printing again.

Nothing Prints At All

Oh boy. Diagnosing the problem when a printer doesn't print at *all* can be a real chore. Try the following solutions in order. After trying each suggestion, try printing again. If you still don't have any luck, call WordPerfect Customer Support at 800/541-5170 if you have a laser printer, or 800/541-5160 if you have any other kind of printer. They'll be happy to help you work through the problem.

▼ Make sure that your printer is on, is on-line, and has paper in it. Also, make sure that the cable that connects your printer to your computer is firmly connected. If you're not sure which cable this is, hunt down somebody who likes to fiddle with computers and ask him.

▼ Clear out your printer queue. Do this by pressing Shift-F7, C to go to printer control. Press C to cancel your print jobs, and then press the asterisk (*) to tell WordPerfect to clear out all the print jobs. Look at the instructions by Action: (the eighth line down from the menu). If this line tells you to press G to reset your computer, press G. You might need to press it a couple times. Press F7 to return to your document screen.

▼ Go to a blank document screen, type a few words, and try to print them. If they print, something's wrong with your document. To fix the problem, clear the document screen, and then retrieve the document that you had trouble printing. Go to the top of the document (you do this by pressing Home, Home, up-arrow key), turn on Block by pressing Alt-F4, and then go to the bottom of the document (Home, Home, down-arrow key). Delete the block (this is temporary, I promise) by pressing Delete, Y. Press F7, N, N to clear your document screen. Press F1, 1 to magically restore your document to the screen. Try printing it again.

▼ Leave WordPerfect and try printing from another program. If you can't print from *any* of your programs, there's a problem with either the printer, the cable, or your computer.

▼ Turn off your printer, wait for a few seconds, and then turn on the printer again. Sometimes printers can crash, just like your computer does. By turning the thing off and back on, you clear the printer's memory.

Printing a Few Pages

You don't have to print the entire document. In some cases, you might just want to print a few pages. Or just one page. Or just one paragraph. WordPerfect can accommodate you.

To print only certain pages from your document, make sure that your printer is set up and the document is on-screen. Press Shift-F7 to make the Print menu appear. Then press M to print multiple pages.

You see this prompt at the bottom of the screen:

    Page(s):

Type the page numbers you want to print; then press Enter. WordPerfect returns to the document screen and only the pages you specified are printed. (This procedure works even if you didn't add page numbers to the document.)

Checklist

▼ If you want to print from one page to another, type the first page to be printed, a dash, and then the last page to be printed. For example, if you want to print from page three to page eight, type **3-8**.

▼ You can also print individual pages. To do this, type each page number to be printed, separated by commas. For example, if you want to print pages 4, 9, and 12, type **4,9,12**.

▼ You can combine the two ways of printing certain pages. For example, if you want to print pages 1 through 3, as well as pages 8 and 10, type **1-3,8,10**.

▼ If you want to print from the beginning of the document to a certain page, type a dash, and then type the last page you want. For example, if you want to print from the beginning of the document to page 13, type **-13**.

▼ You can print from a certain page to the end of the document by typing the page number followed by a dash. For example, if you want to print from page 8 to the end of the document, type **8-**.

Print Just One Page

If you only need one page of it, just print one page of it. Move your cursor to the page you want to print. It doesn't matter where the cursor is

on the page: it can be at the top, bottom, or anywhere in between. You might want to check Pg status line (bottom right corner) to be sure that you've got the cursor on the right page.

After you're on the right page, press Shift-F7 to display the Print menu. Press P for Page. WordPerfect returns you to the document screen and prints the page.

Printing Just a Block of Text

Suppose that you don't even want to print an entire page; you just want to print a paragraph or two—or a single sentence. If that's the case, move the cursor to the beginning of the block that you want to print, press Alt-F4, and then move the cursor to the end point of the block. As you move the cursor, the text you want to print is highlighted. Press Shift-F7. WordPerfect asks

```
Print block? No (Yes)
```

Press Y for Yes.

Printing Your Document Several Times

If you like your document enough to want to pass it out to friends, co-workers, and people you meet waiting for the subway, you can print multiple copies.

TIP

If you have a photocopier handy, use it—rather than your printer—to make the copies. Photocopiers are faster and cost less per page than running multiple copies off your printer. Plus, using a photocopier saves wear and tear on the printer.

Here's how you print several copies of a document:

1. Make sure that the document you want to print is on-screen.

2. Press Shift-F7. The Print menu appears.

3. Press N for Number of Copies. The cursor moves under the number that follows the words Number of Copies.

4. Type the number of copies you want; then press Enter.

The printing doesn't start yet. You've got a couple more decisions to make.

5. Press U for Multiple Copies Generated By. You see this prompt at the bottom of the screen:

```
Multiple Copies Generated by: 1 WordPerfect;
2 Printer: 2
```

If you choose 1 for WordPerfect, the copies will be collated but will come out slower. (*Collated* means that one whole copy of the document—from the first to the last page—is printed, and then another whole copy of the document is printed, and so on.)

If you press 2 for Printer, the copies may come out more quickly, but will not be collated; instead, all the page 1s will print, then all the page 2s will print, and so on. You'll have to arrange the documents in the proper order (sort of like when you helped your third-grade teacher assemble stacks of handouts).

6. Press 1 or 2.

7. Press F to print the Full Document.

WordPerfect goes back to the document screen, and your printer begins printing... and printing... and printing...

Stopping Documents from Being Printed

(Stop the presses!)

You send your print job, fully expecting the printer to make printing noises, and...nothing. What's going on? Or more to the point, what's not going on? Somewhere along the line, the printer got stuck. You'll have to let WordPerfect know by canceling the print job.

Or maybe you send a long document to the printer and realize, *Hey! I don't want to print that document. What was I thinking?*

You can cancel print jobs from the Control Printer screen. Here's how:

1. Press Shift-F7 to bring up the Print menu; then press C for Control Printer.

A screenful of information, vaguely resembling NASA control center, appears.

2. Press C for Cancel Jobs. A question appears at the bottom of the screen:

```
Cancel which job? (*=All Jobs)
```

3. Press the asterisk key (*).

When one print job gets jammed, any other print jobs that come after it have to sit idly by. It's easier to cancel all the print jobs and start over than to try to cancel one job at a time.

Another prompt appears:

```
Cancel all print jobs? No (Yes)
```

4. Press Y for Yes.

WordPerfect tries desperately to clean up the mess, but it may need to ask you a couple of unpredictable questions. If it asks you to press G to continue, press G. If WordPerfect wants to know whether you're sure you want to cancel the print job, press Y for Yes.

Keep answering the questions and following the directions that WordPerfect flings at you. When the screen finally reads None, press F7 to return to your document screen.

TIP

Your printer may have some remnants of the bad print job remaining. To clear everything, cancel the print job, turn off the printer, wait a couple seconds, and then turn on the printer. Your printer should now be cleared of the bad print job.

Setting Up a Printer

If you've just bought a new printer or if you haven't gone through the heart-wrenching process of installing a printer, you need to do so. (It's part of the WordPerfect initiation process.) In techie terms, you need to "install a printer driver." This intimidating task should not be attempted alone by mere mortals.

Instead, butter up a WordPerfect buddy and ask him to do it for you. Or make a call to the Customer Support people at WordPerfect. They'll step you through this complex process. You can call these folks at 800/541-5160. Before you make the call, though, have these things ready:

Checklist

▼ Have the disks that came with WordPerfect on hand. You'll need at least some of them.

▼ Know the name of your printer, including the make and model. It's not good enough to know just the type of printer. You need to know who made it and what model it is. On most printers, the name (make and model) of the printer is stamped on the printer.

▼ Be at your computer when you make the phone call.

▼ Know which directory your WordPerfect program is kept in, such as C:\WP51.

CHAPTER 14

Working with Documents

(WordPerfect's Answer to the Overstuffed Filing Cabinet)

IN A NUTSHELL

▼ Decipher DOS path names
▼ Display a list of files
▼ View a document before retrieving it
▼ Retrieve a file for editing
▼ Find files
▼ Print a single document
▼ Print many documents
▼ Delete files you don't need any longer
▼ Create directories
▼ Change directories
▼ Copy files
▼ Move files from one directory to another

When you work with WordPerfect, you've got to learn some thing about managing files. *Files* are the documents you've named and put on your hard disk (and floppy disks, too). They're sitting on your hard disk right now, seemingly multiplying at a furious rate. To keep them from getting out of control, you're going to have to pay them a little attention.

To begin, you need a small dose of DOS. This chapter starts by explaining *paths* and *directories*, as they relate to files. You probably should read this section.

Then this chapter covers the stuff you can do to a file: retrieve it, print it, delete it, curl it, clip it, brush it, snip it. Skim the heads to find procedures that interest you. File management isn't a daily task, but it is something you should know how to do.

Files, Directories, and Paths! Oh My!

Files are the individual documents you store on a disk. Rather than lump all files in one pile on the hard disk, you can—and should—divide the hard disk into sections. These sections are called *directories*.

One main directory, called the *root directory*, houses all the other directories. You can have many directories within the root directory. And you can have directories within directories within directories. (Sometimes the term *subdirectory* rather than *directory* is used; a subdirectory is a directory that is nested under another directory. The two terms mean the same thing.)

BUZZWORDS

DIRECTORY
A *directory* is a section of your hard disk. If your hard disk is an entire house, a directory is one room. The path tells you how to get to that room: Go through the dining room to the kitchen.

The route through all the directories is called the *path*. For instance, decode this path:

    C:\WP51\DATA\COOKIE.DOC

▼ C: indicates the drive (here, drive C).

▼ \ (backslash) is the name of the root directory.

▼ WP51 is the first directory.

▼ DATA is a directory within WP51.

▼ COOKIE.DOC is the file name.

Why is all this important? When you start to organize your files into directories and you can't find a file you are sure you saved, you'll need some clues to decode the path and the directory structure.

Starting List Files

(Unlock the file cabinet)

WordPerfect's List Files feature does just what its name implies: it lists files. After you see the file list on-screen, you can select the file you want and then retrieve it, print it, copy it—whatever you want.

To display a list of files, follow these steps:

1. Press F5.

A prompt appears at the bottom of the screen, something like this:

    Dir C:\WP51\DOCS*.*

This prompt tells you what directory you're about to look at.

2. Press Enter.

The List Files screen comes up.

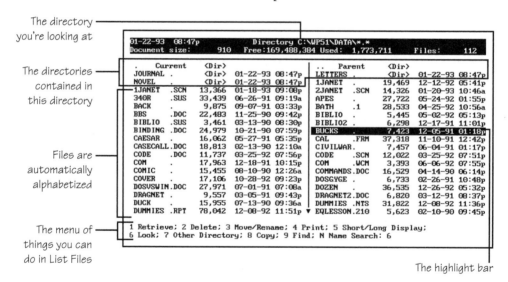

The directory you're looking at

The directories contained in this directory

Files are automatically alphabetized

The menu of things you can do in List Files

The highlight bar

Checklist

▼ Directories are at the top and have a `<Dir>` to the right of the directory name. The directories you see are housed in the directory you're currently listing.

▼ Files are sorted alphabetically in List Files. Files are listed in two columns, and they're sorted from left to right.

▼ The file names, at the left side of each column, are the most important part of the stuff on each line. The other numeric information is how big the file is and when you last worked on it. You'll hardly ever look at those numbers.

▼ When you're in List Files, you move a highlight bar to select the file (or files) you need to do something with (like print, move, or delete). Use the arrow keys and the Page Up and Page Down keys to move the highlight bar. You can move to the bottom of the list by pressing Home, Home, down-arrow key; move to the top of the list by pressing Home, Home, up-arrow key.

▼ When you want to leave List Files, press F7.

TIP

If you want a printout of your files, press Shift-F7 while you're in the List Files screen.

Preview a Document

(The Peeping Tom feature)

You've managed to get into List Files (F5, Enter). You've got a document highlighted. You even think it's the one you want to work on—but you're not sure. If only you could take a look at the file. With WordPerfect, you can.

To peek at the file (the Look feature), simply highlight the file in List Files and press Enter.

▼ When you're finished looking at the document, press Enter to go back to the List Files screen.

▼ If the first screenful of the document isn't enough to tell for sure whether you've got the right file, press Page Down to see another screenful of text. You can keep doing this through the whole document, if that's the kind of thing you enjoy.

▼ You can't edit the document in Look.

▼ The Look feature is good, but it's not exact. It can't display things like graphics, tables, and some text emphasizers, like italic.

▼ If you find that the document you're looking at isn't the one you need, you can look at the next or previous document just by pressing N (for Next) or P (for Previous).

Retrieve a Document

The main reason you use List Files is to retrieve a document you need. To retrieve a document, start from a blank document screen. Then go to List Files (press F5, Enter). After you're in List Files, do this:

1. Highlight the file you want.

2. Press R for Retrieve.

The document appears on-screen, and you're ready to go.

EXPERTS ONLY

The document combo platter

Once in a while, you might want to insert one document into another document. Begin by retrieving the first document. Move the cursor to where you want to insert the second document. Press F5, Enter to go back into List Files. Highlight the document you want to insert, and press R for Retrieve. A message appears on-screen:

```
Retrieve into current document? No (Yes)
```

Press Y to combine the two documents. You should then save the combined document with a new name.

Selecting a File Name Quickly

Before long, you'll have hundreds of documents. When that happens, it gets to be a real nuisance to use your arrow keys to highlight the one particular file you need...especially when the file starts with a V or some other letter far down in the alphabet.

You can speed up the process by using the Name Search feature of List Files. Here's how:

1. From the List Files screen, press N for Name search.

2. Press the first character of the file you're looking for.

WordPerfect quickly jumps down to the first file that begins with that letter (or number). You can continue typing the file name and WordPerfect keeps searching for the closest match to those letters.

3. After you find the file, press Enter (or any of the arrow keys) to turn off Name Search.

4. Press R to retrieve the document.

Checklist

▼ If you make a typo while using Name Search, press Backspace to erase characters; then retype the characters.

▼ One of the most common mistakes when using Name Search is to forget to turn it off after you find the file you want. If you highlight a file by using Name Search and then try to do something with that file—such as press R for Retrieve—Name Search starts looking for a different file. Press Backspace to go back to the file you want, and then press Enter to turn off Name Search.

What's Its Name?

When you haven't used a file in a while, you forget its name. It's often easier to remember certain words you used frequently in the document than to remember the actual name of the document. Fortunately for you, WordPerfect will search through your files for text that you specify, and then tell you what files contain the text.

To look for files that contain certain words, you need to be in List Files (F5, Enter). Then follow these steps:

1. Press F for Find.

   WordPerfect shows this menu:

   ```
   Find: 1 Name; 2 Doc Summary; 3 First Pg; 4 Entire Doc;
   5 Conditions; 6 Undo: 0
   ```

You want WordPerfect to search through all of the documents.

2. Press E for Entire Document.

Now WordPerfect wants you to tell it what word or phrase to search for. It shows this prompt:

```
Word pattern:
```

3. Type the word you want WordPerfect to look for; then press Enter.

Actually, you can type more than one word if you like, but most people get best results if they keep it to just one word. Use a word that you're sure has something to do with the file you're using. For instance, if you've just written a Master's thesis on armadillo farms, the word **armadillo** is a safe bet.

WordPerfect shows the List Files screen again, but this time the screen lists only the files that contain the word you specified. You should be able to find the file you want from this narrowed list.

Checklist

▼ If you're still not sure which file is the one you're looking for, highlight one you think is right and use the Look feature. (The section "Preview a Document" earlier in this chapter explains the Look feature.) Preview the files in the list until you find the one you need.

▼ After you find the file, you probably want to print it or retrieve it. Highlight the file; then press P to print the document, or R to retrieve it.

▼ If you've got a lot of documents in the directory, WordPerfect might take several minutes to search all the files. Give yourself a few minutes when you start this process.

Printing a Document from List Files

(Avoid the middleman)

When it comes right down to it, the main reason you use WordPerfect is to get your words onto paper. List Files lets you print your documents without having to go through the hassle of retrieving them first.

To print a document from the List Files screen, first make sure that your printer is on and set to print. Then follow these steps:

1. Highlight the file you want to print.

2. Press P for Print.

A prompt appears at the bottom of the screen:

```
Pages: (All)
```

3. Press Enter.

The document is printed.

Printing File after File after File

If you want to print several files—all the chapters in your Great American Novel—you can mark them and then print them. Here's how:

1. Go to List Files (F5, Enter).

2. Move the highlight bar to one of the files you want to print.

3. Press the asterisk key (it's the Shift-8 character on your keyboard and looks like this: *). An asterisk appears beside the file. This is called *marking* the file.

If you mark a file you don't want to print after all, move the highlight bar back onto the file and press the asterisk (*) again. This unmarks the file. If you want to unmark all the marked files, press Alt-F5.

4. Mark the other files you want to print.

5. Press P for Print.

A prompt appears:

```
Print marked files? No (Yes)
```

6. Press Y.

The Pages: prompt appears.

7. Press Enter to accept All.

Deleting a File

Murphy's Law: The minute after you delete a file, you'll need it. Granted, you *do* want to erase files from time to time; it keeps your hard disk from getting cluttered. But be careful! If you even *suspect* that you might need a document sometime in the future, don't erase it.

Now that I've got you too scared to ever delete anything, here are the steps to erase a document you no longer need:

1. Start List Files (F5, Enter) and highlight the file to delete.

2. Press D.

 A prompt appears:

 ```
 Delete filename? No (Yes)
 ```

3. Press Y for Yes.

The file's gone. I hope you don't need it in ten minutes.

Deleting for Serious Hard Disk Housecleaning

If you're really in the mood for some zealous housekeeping, you can delete a whole bunch of files at once. In List Files (F5, Enter), highlight a file you don't need, and then press the asterisk (*) key—Shift-8. That marks the file for death.

Mark other files you want to get rid of. If you accidentally mark a file and want to unmark it, highlight the file and press the asterisk key again. When you've marked all the files you want to delete, press D. WordPerfect asks

```
Delete marked files? No (Yes)
```

Press Y for Yes. Just to be sure, WordPerfect asks the same question again, phrased a little differently:

```
Marked files will be deleted.  Continue? No (Yes)
```

Again, press Y for Yes.

Doing the Directory Thing

(For organizational nuts)

If you are an organizational fanatic, you may want to set up directories for different types of documents: one for reports, one for memos, one for letters to Uncle Dale. In this case, read the rest of this chapter to learn about the wonderful world of directories.

If you aren't into directories, you can skip the rest of this chapter. You won't need to do the directory hop.

Creating a New Directory

Few things in life make you feel so organized and purposeful as when you create a new directory for a certain type of document. After all, out of the chaos of the hard disk you've made an organized home for a specific type of file, like letters or memos.

The nice thing about creating new directories in WordPerfect is that it's easy. Just follow these steps from a document screen:

1. Press F5, and then press = (the equal sign).

A prompt appears, asking you to type a new directory.

2. Type the path of the directory you want to create.

For example, if you want a LETTERS\ directory in your C:\WP51\DOCS\ directory, type **C:\WP51\DOCS\LETTERS**.

3. Press Enter.

A new prompt appears, asking whether you *really* want to create this new directory:

```
Create C:\WP51\DATA\LETTERS? No (Yes)
```

4. Press Y for Yes.

The prompt disappears and you're back at the document screen, but the directory is created.

Checklist

▼ If you're already in the List Files screen and want to create a new directory, press O for Other Directory; then follow steps 2 through 4. You'll end up back at List Files—not the document screen—after creating the directory.

▼ The directories you create must be in directories that already exist. You can't create a C:\DREAMS\STRANGE\ directory unless the C:\DREAMS\ directory already exists. You would need to create a C:\DREAMS\ directory, and then put the STRANGE\ directory inside it.

▼ Directory names follow the same rules as file names: they should be eight or fewer characters, and use only letters and numbers. If you make your directory names short—six or fewer characters—you don't have to type as much when you want to move from one directory to the next.

Moving around Directories

If you've taken the plunge and created a whole bevy of directories you want to keep various types of documents in, you need to know how to move from one directory to the other.

Go to List Files by pressing F5, Enter. At the top of the list (just below where it reads `Current` and `Parent`) you see all the directories within the current directory. (Incidentally, directories have a `<Dir>`, whereas files have a number.)

Go to a directory

To go to one of the listed directories, move your highlight bar to that directory, and then press Enter twice. For example, suppose that you're in the C:\WP51\DOCS\ directory, but you want to be in the C:\WP51\DOCS\LETTERS\ directory. Just move the highlight bar to LETTERS and press Enter twice. Easy.

Go from a directory to its parent directory

How about when you want to move back a level? Say, for example, you're in List Files and want to move from C:\WP51\DOCS\LETTERS\ to C:\WP51\DOCS\. Just highlight the *parent* directory (at the top of the list, on the right side of the screen), and then press Enter twice.

BUZZWORDS

PARENT DIRECTORY

For some reason known only to a few key programmers, a directory that contains another directory is called a parent directory. So, C:\WP51\ is the parent directory to C:\WP51\DATA.

Go to a different drive

To list files on a floppy disk, first insert the disk and press F5. Then type **A:** and press Enter to display files on drive A. Type **B:** and press Enter to display files on drive B. To display files on drive C again, type **C:** and press Enter.

Go from one directory to a completely different directory

Sometimes you'll want to go to a completely nonrelated directory such as the directory for a different program. Or you might want to go to a different disk, such as one of your floppy disks. Start at a document screen or from List Files; then follow these directions:

1. Press F5.

A prompt appears at the bottom of your screen, something like this:

```
Dir C:\WP51\DATA\*.*
```

2. In List Files, type the path to the directory you want to see.

As you begin typing, the old path disappears, replaced by your new one. For example, if you want to see the list of files in the POLICIES directory on drive C, type **C:\POLICIES**.

3. Press Enter.

The list of files appears.

▼ If you type a path that doesn't exist, WordPerfect still goes into List Files, but no files will appear. Press F7 and try again, making sure you type the name of a path that really exists.

▼ Another, nastier way WordPerfect might let you know you've typed your path wrong is to quickly flash `Invalid drive/path specification` on-screen. Try again, typing very carefully.

Copying Files

(The file photocopier)

In this wondrous computer age, people trade computer files like they used to trade baseball cards. Here's how you copy a file:

1. Start List Files by pressing F5, Enter.

2. Move to the directory that has the files you want to copy.

3. Highlight the file you want to copy.

4. Press C for Copy.

A prompt appears at the bottom of the screen:

```
Copy this file to:
```

5. Type the path where you want a copy of the file; then press Enter.

For example, you might type **C:\WP51\DOCS**.

The file is copied to the directory you specify.

▼ If a file by the same name already exists in the directory you're copying to, WordPerfect asks whether you want to replace the existing file. Only press Y (for Yes) if you *really* want to get rid of the file that's already there.

▼ When you type the path you want to copy the file to, you can also type a different file name at the end of the path. The file is copied to the new directory, but it has the new name you specify.

Massive File Copying

List Files is handy when you need to copy several files from one drive or directory to another. Here's how:

1. Start List Files by pressing F5, Enter.

2. Move to the directory that has the files you want to copy.

3. Mark the files you want to copy.

You *mark* a file by highlighting that file, and then pressing the asterisk (*) key—Shift-8 on most keyboards. The file you highlighted then has an asterisk to its left, which means it's *marked*.

If you need, you can unmark files by highlighting them again and pressing the asterisk key again.

4. Press C for Copy.

WordPerfect asks:

```
Copy marked files? No (Yes)
```

5. Press Y for Yes.

Now WordPerfect wants to know where you want to copy the files to:

```
Copy all marked files to:
```

6. Type the path where you want the copies of the files; then press Enter.

Be sure to type the full path, such as **C:\WP51\DOCS**.

If WordPerfect asks a question like `Replace filename?`, you've already got a file by that name. Press N for No unless you're *absolutely* sure you want to replace the old file with the one you're copying. If you want to replace the old file, press Y for Yes.

7. Press F7 to leave List Files.

Your files are copied.

Moving Files

When you're ready to roll up your sleeves and do some serious hard disk housecleaning, List Files' Move feature can be a big help. It moves files

from one place to another. For instance, you might want to move all the chapters of your Great American Novel into their own directory. Here's how you do it:

1. Press F5, Enter to start List Files.

2. Move to the directory that has the files you want to move.

3. Highlight the file you want to move.

4. Press M for Move/Rename.

WordPerfect asks where you want to move the file to:

        New Name:

5. Type the path you want the file to go to, such as C:\WP51\DOCS\LETTERS\. Then press Enter.

Checklist

▼ You can type a different file name after the path name, such as C:\WP51\DOCS\LETTERS\NEWNAME.DOC. This moves *and* renames the document.

▼ If you want to only change the document's name, just type a new file name. Don't type a path. WordPerfect will rename the file and leave it in the current directory.

PART V

Impressive Stuff

Includes:

CHAPTER 15

Using Lines in Your Documents

(Line Up!)

In A Nutshell

▼ Create horizontal lines
▼ Create vertical lines

One of the easiest ways to give your pages a little pizzazz is to strategically place lines on the page. Horizontal lines at the top and bottom of the page give documents a classy, typeset look. A vertical line can set one column of information off from another. You can also use lines to create unique designs that you can then sell for lots of money at local art shows. Or you can use them like this:

Horizontal
line →

Vertical line →

Starr Madding
Actress • Singer • Dancer • Waitress
509 East 52nd Street, #3G • New York, NY • 00098   Phone (382) 555-5555

Objective

To secure a lucrative position in either the entertainment or food services industry.

Education

Received diploma from Mott High School, Waterford, Michigan

Graduated with honors from two-week advanced course at Baker Bartending School, Indianapolis, Indiana

Successfully completed two semesters of training at Farling Beauty College, Muncie, Indiana

Experience

Nick's Cafe Russiana, September 1980 to present.
• Serve patrons food and drinks.
• Highest tip recipient on staff due to my pleasant personality and choice of attire.
• Often perform rendition of "The Rose" during weekly karoke night.
• Accidentally spilled wine on Casey Kasem, who enthusiastically promised me that I could "go places in this town."

Back of head seen prominently in ferris wheel scene of *Rocky VII*.

Played one of background crew people for Burger King "Hold the Pickle, Hold the Lettuce" stint.

Portrayed "Angry Girl In Phone Booth" in *Physical Evidence*.

Very close to getting part of show girl in *Graffiti Bridge*.

Rode up three floors on elevator with Aidan Quinn during Bloomingdale's 14-hour sale.

Making Horizontal Lines

(On the horizon)

Horizontal lines are great for separating headers and footers from the rest of the document. They're useful in resumes for separating your name and address from the body of the text. They're also perfect to use if you want to show the brain activity of a rutabaga.

To create a horizontal (left-to-right) line, move the cursor to where you want the line. Press Alt-F9. Alt-F9 is the Graphics key, and lines are considered part of graphics. This menu appears at the bottom of your screen:

```
1 Figure; 2 Table Box; 3 Text Box; 4 User Box; 5 Line;
6 Equation: 0
```

Press L. Another menu comes up:

```
Create Line: 1 Horizontal; 2 Vertical; Edit Line:
3 Horizontal; 4 Vertical: 0
```

Press H. This time, the full-blown Graphics: Horizontal Line menu appears. Press F7 to create the line with the default settings. (The default settings create a thin, solid black line that extends from the left to the right margin.)

You can't see the horizontal line you just created, but it's there. If you want to take a peek, use the View Document feature. (Flip back to Chapter 6 if you can't remember how to use this feature.)

▼ If you want a line to separate your header from the rest of the document, put the line *inside* the header. While you're in the header edit screen, create the header. (See Chapter 11 for all the dirt on creating headers.) Then press Home, Home, down-arrow key; press Enter to go to a new line; and then follow the steps to make the line. Press F7 twice to return to the document screen.

▼ To use a line to separate a footer from the rest of the document, you'd want the line at the *top* of the text, requiring Home, Home, up-arrow key.

▼ If you want to change the thickness of the line from the Graphics: Horizontal Line menu, press W for Width of Line. Type the thickness you want for the line, using decimal values. A good medium thickness for lines is 0.05, and a very thick line is 0.1.

▼ Lines are usually black, but you can have them in shades of gray, too. At the Graphics: Horizontal Line menu, press G for gray shading. Type a number from **1-100**. The larger the number, the darker the line.

Making Vertical Lines

Horizontal lines are more popular and useful then their counterpart, vertical lines. Still you might find a place for them in your document. For instance, if you use columns, you can put a vertical line between the columns.

To create a vertical line, start by pressing Alt-F9. The Graphics menu appears:

```
1 Figure; 2 Table Box; 3 Text Box; 4 User Box; 5 Line;
6 Equation: 0
```

Press L to create a line. Now the Line-creation menu comes up:

```
Create Line: 1 Horizontal; 2 Vertical; Edit Line:
3 Horizontal; 4 Vertical: 0
```

Press V to create a vertical line. The Graphics: Vertical Line menu appears. This menu isn't that much different from the Graphics: Horizontal Line menu.

The default line WordPerfect creates is a thin line going from the top margin to the bottom, on the left side of the page. If that's what you want, press F7.

Changing the Line's Placement on the Page

To change the position of the vertical line at the Graphics: Horizontal Line menu, press H for Horizontal Position. Then press R (for Right) to align the line at the right margin. Or press S (for Set Position) and type the distance—in inches—that you want the vertical line to appear from the left edge of the paper. Press Enter and the lines jump to their new position.

Changing the Length of the Line

If you want to change the length of the line, press V for Vertical Position. Then do one of the following:

▼ Press F to extend the line from the top margin to the bottom margin.

▼ Press T to start the line at the top of the page. Next, press L for Length of line, type how long you want the line to be, and press Enter.

▼ Press C to center the line between the top and bottom of the page. Next press L for Length of line, type the length of the line you want, and press Enter.

▼ Press B if you want the line to go to the bottom margin. Then press L for Length of line, type how far up from the bottom margin you want the line to extend, and press Enter.

▼ Press S for Set Position if you want the top of the line to be at some specific height. Next, type how far from the top of the page you want the line to begin, and press Enter. Now tell WordPerfect how long you want the line to be by pressing L for Length of Line, typing the length of the line you need, and pressing Enter.

EXPERTS ONLY

Use columns?

Vertical lines look groovy when placed between columns. (Look at Chapter 17 if you want to create columns.) First, place the cursor somewhere in one of the columns. At the Graphics: Vertical Line, press B for Between Columns. You are asked where to place the line. Type the number of the column that you want to be left of your line. (The line will be to the right of the column.) If you want a line between columns 2 and 3, for example, you would type **2**.

CAUTION

If you want a border around the page, don't do it with lines. Instead, see Chapter 16. This chapter teaches you the trick of adding a border to an entire page.

Removing Lines

Those graphic lines look great, but they can be pesky when you want to change them or remove them. Why? Well, you can't see the line in your document. So you have to peek at Reveal Codes to find the line code.

To get rid of a line, move the cursor somewhere near the place in the document where the line appears. Then press Alt-F3 to turn on Reveal Codes. (If the screen now scares you, go back to Chapter 12, which explains all about Reveal Codes.) Look around for the [HLine] or [VLine] code. To delete the line, put the cursor on the code and press Delete. Turn off Reveal Codes by pressing Alt-F3.

TIP

If you can't find the line, you can search for it. Press F2. Then press Alt-F9, L, and either H (horizontal line) or V (vertical line). To start the search, press F2. The cursor moves so that it's positioned right after the code that creates the line. Press Backspace (and Y, if Reveal Codes is off) to delete the line.

CHAPTER 16

Using Graphics in Your Documents

(Pretty as a Picture)

IN A NUTSHELL

▼ Put a graphic into your document

▼ Put a border around a page

I HATE WORDPERFECT!

This chapter shows you how to add pictures (called *graphics* in computer lingo) to your document. You can add a flag to your Race Day party invitation. Or add a trophy to your Bowling League newsletter. Friends and enemies alike will be in awe of your computer prowess.

M E M O R A N D U M

DATE: 4/6/93

FROM: THE BIG BOSS

TO: ALL EMPLOYEES

SUBJECT: WASTING TIME

I have recently noticed that several of you have been coming in to work at 11:45, working for as little as three minutes, then taking off for an early lunch. Further, these early lunches have been lasting for up to two and a half hours.

When you manage to get back to work, I hear sounds coming from your offices. Not sounds of people busily typing and trying to make up for lost time, but of beeps and explosion noises that could only come from video games, namely "Killer Mutant Alien Cockroaches From Planet Yech."

I'm a reasonable person, and can understand occasional tardiness. However, I'm immensely disappointed that none of you have been able to get past level 12 at the video game. If I don't hear soon of one of you destroying the Great Skull Of Doom, there will be hell to pay.

A WordPerfect document with a graphics file (CLOCK.WPG) to liven things up.

CHAPTER 16

Graphics is a topic unto itself. This chapter is only a snapshot. For everything you care to know about graphics, consider picking up another Que book, *Using WordPerfect 5.1*, Special Edition.

Can I Insert a Drawing of My Dog?

You can't create graphics in WordPerfect. Instead, you use pre-fab graphics. These graphics are stored in a file on disk. Quite a few come with WordPerfect. If you want more, more, more, though, most computer stores sell packages of graphics files (called *clip art*) on a wide range of topics.

TIP

If you purchase a clip art package, make sure that the graphics format is compatible with WordPerfect (most are). Also, be aware that the quality of clip art images can vary from very good to very poor. Ask the salesperson to show you some samples printed from WordPerfect.

BUZZWORDS

CLIP ART

Clip art is just any drawing or picture that's saved in a computerized format. You can add clip art to documents to snazz up the documents.

Using Graphics in Documents

(A picture is worth...)

There are lots of options for graphics. Do you want to mess with most of them? No. Instead, you can pop in a graphic in the default location. Here's how:

1. Decide what graphics file you want to use.

Graphics files have file names, just like documents do. You can locate the file names of graphics by looking at the "Graphic Images" appendix in your WordPerfect manual. The name of the file is under the picture of the graphic. Make a note of the graphic file name you want to use. If you can't find the manual, you can find a good graphic by trial and error.

2. Move your cursor to the top of the page where you want the graphic.

The position of the cursor in the page isn't really that critical, but the top of the page is a nice, neat place to put codes.

3. Press Alt-F9, F for Figure, and then C for Create.

Each of these keys brings up a menu, which is all part of the complexity you want to avoid. Any time you want to put a graphic in your document, these keys will take you to the right place—the Definition: Figure menu. The menu looks like this:

```
Definition: Figure
      1 - Filename
      2 - Contents              Empty
      3 - Caption
      4 - Anchor Type           Paragraph
      5 - Vertical Position     0"
      6 - Horizontal Position   Right
      7 - Size                  3.25" wide x 3.25" (high)
      8 - Wrap Text Around Box  Yes
      9 - Edit



Selection: 0
```

*The Definition:
Figure menu*

4. Press F for Filename.

This prompt appears at the bottom of the screen:

```
Enter filename:                              (List Files)
```

5. If you know the name of the file, type it and press Enter.

If you don't know the name of the file, press F5, Enter to display the List Files screen. From this list, highlight the .WPG file you want and press R for Retrieve. Generally, it doesn't take a genius to look at the file name and figure out what the picture shows. For instance, BALLOONS shows some balloons!

6. Press F7 to return to the document screen.

On-screen, in the upper right corner, you see the outline of a box. This box represents the graphic. To see the graphic, you have to preview the document (press Shift-F7, then V).

TIP

> When you're in the Definition: Figure menu, you can get a sneak preview of how the graphic looks. Press E for Edit. The graphic appears. When you finish oohing and aahing over the figure, press F7 to go back to the Definition: Figure menu.

Checklist

▼ WordPerfect automatically wraps text around your graphic. You don't have to worry about your document writing over the top of a graphic.

▼ You can do much more with the graphic: change its size, change its placement on the page, and on and on. Try experimenting. Or get a bigger, fatter, more expensive book on WordPerfect like, for instance, *Using WordPerfect 5.1*, Special Edition, published by Que. (Well, say, Que also published the book you're reading now; what a coincidence.)

▼ Graphics look their best when you print them at high resolution. When you want to print a document that contains graphics, press Shift-F7. At the Print menu, press G for Graphics Quality, and H for High. You can then continue printing as you normally do.

▼ If you change your mind and don't want to insert the graphic, press F1 from the Definition Figure menu to cancel. You have to do this before you press F7 to return to the document.

▼ If you don't like the graphic, delete it. Press Alt-F3 to turn on Reveal Codes. Highlight the code [Fig Box :1] and press Delete. Press Alt-F3 again to turn off Reveal Codes.

▼ If you get a `File Not Found` message when you type the name, try typing the name again. Be sure you type it correctly and be sure that you type the extension. If you get the same message a second time, use the List Files feature by pressing F5, Enter at the `Enter filename` prompt.

Using Graphics to Make a Page Border

(Boxing things in)

Occasionally, you might want to put a border around your page, to draw a little extra attention to your document. If you need to make your document fancy and are willing to follow a dozen steps, read on. If you aren't interested, skip it.

June 18, 1993

824 Rosedale Ct.
Grand Junction, CO 81001

Steven Schmallegar, President
New Moose Cinema, Inc.
468 S. Nixon Blvd.
Orange, CA 82599

Dear Mr. Schmallegar:

I understand that your company is currently shopping around for new scripts. I think I have something you'll like. What I mean to say is, I *know* I have it, but I think you'll like it, if you take my meaning.

I have written a screenplay based on Fyodor Dostoevsky's famous whodunnit novel *Crime And Punishment*. I know, I know, that's not exactly a new idea. But here's the twist, Mr. Schmallegar, and I think you'll agree that this is new: *It's a musical.*

"Why a musical?" you're certainly entitled to ask. Well, I've always thought that the play is just too darn dark, not to mention esoteric, for most people. Sure they want culture, but they also want entertainment—something that'll put a little bounce in their step.

Imagine Raskolnikov as he contemplates murdering the old pawnshop woman. Instead of just stewing and muttering to himself, he breaks into song, something that both conveys his inner turmoil *and* makes us want to tap our toes.

I could go on and on, Mr. Schmallegar, but I think you've got the idea. I hope you're as excited about this project as I.

Sincerely,

Howard Beighfey

P.S. Perhaps with the recent successful animated adaptations of various classic stories, we should consider making this an *animated musical*. I look forward to hearing from you.

You can fool WordPerfect into making a border by using the Graphics feature...without a graphic in the box. Here's how:

CAUTION

These steps are designed to work on 8.5-by-11-inch paper with 1-inch margins. Don't use this trick with other sizes or margins—the results will be repulsive.

1. Move the cursor to the top of the page you want a border around.

2. Press Alt-F9, F for Figure, and then C for Create.

This brings you to the Definition: Figure menu, which is where you'll create a border for your page.

3. Press T for Anchor Type, A for Page, 0, and then Enter.

This spiffy little key combination keeps the border on the current page.

4. Press V for Vertical Position, and then S for Set Position.

This prompt appears

```
Offset from top of page:
```

5. Type 0.533 and press Enter.

This is the distance from the top of the page to your top border. It took me most of an afternoon to figure out what number to use, so don't worry about figuring out why I use this number. Just trust me. It works.

6. Press H for Horizontal Position, and then S for Set Position.

Another prompt appears:

```
Offset from left of page:
```

7. Type **0.7**, and then press Enter.

Again, don't worry about why I use this number. It works.

8. Press S for Size, and then B for Set Both.

This following prompt appears:

    Width =

9. Type **7.1**, and then press Enter.

This is the width of your border. Another prompt appears:

    Height =

10. Type **9.6**, and then press Enter.

This number specifies the height of your border.

11. Press W for Wrap Text Around Box; then press N for No.

This step tells WordPerfect to let you type text inside the border.

12. Press F7 to return to the document screen.

You can't see the border, but it's there—just outside your margins. You can see the border by printing your page or by using the Print Preview feature. (Flip back to Chapter 6 if you don't remember how to use Print Preview.)

CHAPTER 17

Using Columns
(Your Own Newspaper)

IN A NUTSHELL

▼ Set up margins to give your columns extra space

▼ Make a headline to go above your columns

▼ Put your document in columns

▼ Create columns

▼ Type the text

Hey, you might get so good at WordPerfect that you want to set up your own press. You can publish a family newsletter, de tailing how the burglary charges against Little Jimmy were dropped and how much happier Pop has been since he got those new dentures. Or you might set up a neighborhood newsletter, or a company newsletter, or a newsletter for cat haters. Anything you want.

You could do a newsletter with one, plain column, but that will just alert your family, neighbors, and coworkers that you are an amateur. Instead use two or three columns and impress your subscribers. This document has three columns:

NEWS FROM THE BRADYS

Volume III, Issue 2   May 12, 1968

WELCOME . . .
To another edition of "News From The Bradys," the newsletter we send to all our friends and family to keep you in touch with what our ultra-normal family is doing.

Before we get started with each of the kids' antics (and believe me, they've been busy this month), I thought I'd respond to all the letters I've recently received asking about that pesky Partridge family that lives down the street.

Yes, they still practice until all hours of the night. Nobody can sleep. June Cleaver, our next door neighbor, has been especially affected by that nasty Danny Partridge's incessant drumming. She's so upset she can't eat and her hands shake. I could tell how bad she's taking all this noise when the other day I heard her shout, "Darn it Ward, how could you have *ever* come up with such a stupid name as "Beaver?!" I wouldn't be surprised if June has to make another trip to the psychiatrist before too long.

Back to the Partridges, though. No, they *still* haven't painted that horrid bus. No, Ms. Partridge *still* can't find

a respectable husband— though I personally think she's in remarkable shape for having had who knows how many children.

And finally, yes, they still have that Reuben Kincaid as their manager. No, I can't figure it out either (unless *he's* the romantic interest, perish the thought). It seems that every time he finds them a gig, it winds up being in a haunted cave, a federal prison or who knows where else. Oh well. Beggars can't be choosers, I suppose.

ONE OTHER NOTE
I keep getting letters from some rather nasty relatives and even a few complete strangers wondering about my past. For those of you who are wondering who my first husband was, it's none of your business.

Now then. Let's see what everybody's been doing!

ABOUT ALICE
What would a Brady Newsletter be without a little bit about everybody's favorite housekeeper/maid/cook/auto mechanic? Yes, of course I mean our very own Alice.

I recently got a call from Richie (you know, the

Cunningham boy just across town who looks so much like his younger brother, Opie). He was wondering whether Alice has a last name. That's a poser of a question if I've ever heard one.

Of course, I put the question directly to Alice and she responded, "Not as far as I know. I'm just here because I make good sandwiches and do a great job of making silly remarks, thereby setting the rest of you up for snappy comebacks." Hmmm. Alice seems a little bitter today.

MARSHA MADNESS
Now, onto our children. This issue, we'll start at the oldest—Marsha—and work down. Although now that I think about it, Greg may actually be our oldest. I can never be sure.

One thing that's been concerning me lately is the company Marsha tends to keep. I've seen her more than once with that nasty Laverne and Shirley. Imagine my humiliation—my eldest (or second eldest, see above) hanging out with a couple of *beer factory* workers. I could just die.

Aside from the company she keeps, Marsha is doing

You can use columns for anything you want, of course, but the most common reason why people venture into the world of columns is because they're creating a newsletter.

Before You Begin

You're ready to type your first story about Uncle Dale and Aunt Dot's vacation to Dollywood. But wait. First, you need to ask a few questions: What kind of margins do you want around the page? Do you want a headline above the columns? How about a header at the top of each page? There are some things you should take care of before you create columns.

Make Small Margins

First, it's a good idea to use smaller margins for a document with several columns than you would for a document with only one column. With the regular 1-inch margins, you wouldn't have much space for the columns themselves. You'll want smaller page margins—probably one-half inch on all four sides.

To change your margins, press Home, Home, up-arrow key to go to the top of the document. Then press Shift-F8 to bring up the Format menu, P for Page, and M for Margins. Next, type the new margins. Type **0.5** for the top margin, press Enter, type **0.5** for the bottom margin, and press Enter again.

Now change the left and right margins. Press Enter to go back to the main Format menu. Press L for Line and then M for Margins. Type **0.5** for the left margin, press Enter, type **0.5** for the right margin, and press Enter again. Press F7 to return to the document screen.

Now you have half-inch margins all the way around, which gives you a lot more room for your columns. The art of changing margins is more fully discussed in Chapter 10.

Making a Headline (Read all about it!)

When you use columns, you usually want a headline or banner (like the name of the newsletter) above them. This is where you can put to work all your knowledge of formatting—making text bigger, badder, bolder. And if you don't have that knowledge, just follow along.

First, go to the top of the document by pressing Home, Home, up-arrow key. Press Shift-F6 to turn on WordPerfect's Center feature. Press Ctrl-F8, S, E to turn on an extra large font for your headline. Type the name of your newsletter or your headline or the name of your master's thesis, or whatever, and then press End to turn off Extra Large.

You can quit here if you like. Or you can add a *subtitle*. Press Enter twice to move the cursor below the title. Type any information you want to appear below and to the left of the title, like the volume and issue number. Press Alt-F6 to move the cursor to the right edge of the page, and then insert the date by pressing Shift-F5, T.

Still want more? If you want to add a line, press Enter to move below the issue number and date. Press Alt-F9, L for Line, H for Horizontal, and then F7 to return to the document screen. This puts a horizontal line at the bottom of your *banner* (the name and subheading of the newsletter). The line doesn't show in your document screen, but it will print. For a line on using lines, read Chapter 15.

Press Enter twice to put some distance between the banner and the body of the document.

Creating the Columns

(Divvying up the page)

After you've taken care of setting up the margins and banner for your document, you're all set to go with the columns. Here's what to do:

1. Move the cursor to where you want the columns to begin—generally after the banner or headline.

2. Press Alt-F7.

This menu appears:

```
1 Columns; 2 Tables; 3 Math: 0
```

3. Press C for Columns.

Another menu pops up:

```
Columns: 1 On; 2 Off; 3 Define: 0
```

Before you can turn on Columns, you need to *define* them.

4. Press D for Define.

This time, a fairly frightening screen appears. Luckily, you can ignore it if you want a two-column format.

5. Press F7 to leave the Text Column Definition screen.

Now you're confronted by a one-line menu at the bottom of the screen:

```
Columns: 1 On; 2 Off; 3 Define: 0
```

6. Press O for On.

If you already have text in your document, it jumps into columns. If you plan to type as you go, the text forms into columns as you type.

"I HATE THIS!"

Column 1 and column 2 are in the same column!

If you have more than two or three columns, WordPerfect has a hard time displaying all of them at once. As you write, your columns may seem to overlap or not have enough space between them. Not to worry, though—they'll print just fine.

TIP

Limit yourself to no more than three or four columns. Otherwise, the columns start getting very narrow so that only one or two words fits on a line.

Typing the Text

The final step in creating your newsletter is typing the text. Just type away. You can move, copy, delete, make bold, and do everything you can do in a "normal" (one-column) document. The only difference is how the text flows. When you get to the bottom of one column, WordPerfect takes you to the top of the next one. When you get to the bottom of the last column on a page, WordPerfect takes you to the beginning of the first column on the next page.

238

▼ If you are only part-way down a column, but you want to end that column and begin the next one, press Ctrl-Enter. The cursor jumps to the beginning of the next column.

▼ To move the cursor right one column, press Alt-right arrow key. To move left one column, press Alt-left arrow key. Those keys don't work on some older keyboards, in which case you need to press Ctrl-Home, left-arrow key to move left one column. Likewise, press Ctrl-Home, right-arrow key to move right one column.

▼ If you don't like the text in columns and long for the old one-column format, turn on Reveal Codes (press Alt-F3), delete the [Col Def] code. Then press Alt-F3 again to turn off Reveal Codes.

CHAPTER 18

Using Tables
(Setting the Table)

IN A NUTSHELL

- ▼ Create a table
- ▼ Type text into a table
- ▼ Change the column width
- ▼ Add rows to a table
- ▼ Remove rows from a table
- ▼ Add a border around a paragraph

reating a table without a special table feature is a nightmare. If you've ever typed a table, you know what I mean. You type the first column and then tab to move to the second column. You type the text for that column, but uh-oh, one of the words that is supposed to stay over in column 2 wraps to the next line. You can press Tab to move it in line with the second column, but what if you add text? Then who knows where anything will line up! And what if the second row is longer than the first? You'll have to readjust the second column again.

If you need to organize a lot of information so that it stays in order and is easy to find, it's time you get to know the Tables feature.

The Tables feature lets you organize and categorize information quickly.

Homes For Sale In My Price Range							
Address	Price	Sq. ft	# bedrm	# bath	# car gar.	A/C	Rating
974 W Bernard St	94,000	1480	3	2	2	Yes	***
8201 Hooligan Rd	88,900	1200	2	1.5	1	Yes	**
46 Townshend Circle	96,200	1360	3	2.5	2	Yes	**
232 Peach Street	102,000	1722	4	3	2	Yes	****

This chapter shows you how to make a table *and* make it look good. You also learn how to move around in your table once you've made it.

Creating a Table

Before you dive into the keyboard, punching away madly at keys, you need to do a little planning. First, for the million-dollar question: How many columns do you need? You better get the columns right because adding columns is hard and is not worth covering here. You might also venture a guess at how many rows you need. But it's pretty easy to add or remove extra rows.

BUZZWORDS

CELLS

Tables are composed of columns and rows of cells. A column goes up and down the page. A row goes across. A cell is where the columns and rows cross. A cell looks like a rectangle and is what you type a number or word into.

After you figure out the number of columns you need, you're ready to make the table. Here's what you do:

1. Move the cursor to where you want the table.

Make sure that you move the cursor at the beginning of a blank line.

2. Press Alt-F7.

A menu appears at the bottom of the screen:

```
1 Columns; 2 Tables; 3 Math: 0
```

3. Press T for Tables.

Another menu appears:

```
Table: 1 Create; 2 Edit: 0
```

4. Press C for Create.

WordPerfect asks you how many columns you want:

```
Number of Columns: 3
```

243

The "3" is the *default* number of columns WordPerfect uses for its tables. If you don't specify a number, WordPerfect automatically makes a table that has three columns.

5. Type the number of columns you want; then press Enter.

Now WordPerfect asks you how many rows you want:

    Number of Rows: 1

Sometimes it's not very easy to tell how many rows you want until you've started typing in all the information for your table. Just make a good guess. If you need to add more rows later, you can. If you already know how many rows you need, add two to that number so that you'll have room for the table title and each of the column titles.

6. Type the number of rows you want; then press Enter.

Now a table appears that has a complex menu at the bottom.

The Table Edit menu.

```
Table Edit:  Press Exit when done       Cell A1 Doc 1 Pg 1 Ln 1.14" Pos 1.12"

Ctrl-Arrows Column Widths; Ins Insert; Del Delete; Move Move/Copy;
1 Size; 2 Format; 3 Lines; 4 Header; 5 Math; 6 Options; 7 Join; 8 Split: 0
```

7. Press the down-arrow key to move to the next row in the table.

The cursor (the big rectangle you can move around with your arrow keys) is now on the left side of the second row.

8. Press Ctrl-right arrow key if you want to make this column wider, or Ctrl-left arrow key if you want to make the column narrower.

Keep using these keys until the column is as wide as you want it.

9. Press Tab to move to the next column, then follow step 8 again.

Use this technique to make the columns as wide or narrow as you want them. Don't worry if you're not sure about those widths; you can change them easily later.

10. Press F7 to leave the Table Editor.

The menu disappears, and the table appears in your document screen. Now you're all set to actually start putting your information into your table.

Checklist

▼ While you're in the Table Editor, you can't type text into the table. In fact, all you can do is change the structure of the table. You have to wait until you're out of the Table Editor before you can add text to the table.

▼ Tables can have a huge number of rows, but no more than 32 columns.

▼ If your table will have more than 4 or 5 columns, set narrow left and right margins to make room for all those columns. You learn how to set margins in Chapter 10.

CHAPTER 18

Typing Text into a Table

Now you're all set to type the information that goes into your table. Use your arrow keys to move the cursor into the top row of the table. If you want, press Shift-F6 to make the title centered; then type the table title. The title is centered between the left and right edge of the table.

To type text into the table, move to the cell where you want to add text; then just type the text. Press Tab to move from one cell to the next. To move backward, press Shift-Tab. If you want to move up and down, just use the up- and down-arrow keys.

Checklist

▼ If the text in one cell needs to be more than one line high, WordPerfect automatically makes the row taller to fit any new lines of text.

▼ If you have very narrow columns in your table, you may not be able to fit a whole word or number on a single line, in which case WordPerfect wraps your text to a new line wherever it has to. You can either make the column wider (see the section "Changing Column Width," which is coming up here quickly). Or abbreviate your text to keep it from wrapping in such an odd place, like this:

| ambi |
| dextr |
| ous |

▼ When you move the cursor around the table, the name of the cell shows up in the status line. The columns are lettered—A, B, C, and so on—and are the first name of the cell. The rows are numbered—1, 2, 3, and so on—and are the last name of the cell. The cell name is made up of both the first and last name and looks like A1 or D27.

Changing Column Width

WordPerfect lets you easily make columns narrower or wider. To begin, move the cursor so that it's in that column; then press Alt-F7 to go into the Table Editor. You can now press Ctrl-right arrow key to make the column wider, or Ctrl-left arrow key to make it narrower.

You can only make columns wider or narrower within certain limits— the whole table can't be wider than the page margins. If you want to make one column wider, you may have to make another narrower.

When you're done changing your column widths, press F7 to return to the document screen.

Adding Rows

(One more for the row!)

It's hard to guess the exact number of rows you'll need in a table. You always seem to have just one more item you need to add. Fortunately, adding rows is *no-o-o-o* problem.

To add extra rows to your table, move the cursor so that it's in the row *below* where you want to add the extra rows. It doesn't matter which column the cursor is in. Press Alt-F7 to go into the Table Editor. Press the Insert key. (Sometimes the Insert key just has the word Ins on it. You may have to look around on your keyboard for a minute to find this key.)

This prompt appears at the bottom of the screen:

```
Insert: 1 Rows; 2 Columns: 0
```

Press R for Rows. Now WordPerfect wants to know how many rows you want to add:

```
Number of Rows: 1
```

If you don't tell WordPerfect a specific number, it automatically adds one row.

Type the number of rows you want to add to your table; then press Enter. Press F7 to leave the Table Editor. Now you can fill in your new rows.

TIP

To add a row, move the cursor to the row *below* where you want the new row. Then press Ctrl-Insert. Voilà! A new row is added.

Removing Rows

(One less row to hoe)

Let's say that you enjoy adding rows so much that you go hog-wild and add a bunch more than you need. Now what? Are you stuck with extra rows? No. Just remove them.

Move the cursor so that it's at the top of the rows you want to delete. For example, if you want to delete four blank rows—say, rows 19, 20, 21, and 22—you'd move your cursor so it's in the top of those four rows (row 19). The other three blank rows would be beneath it. It doesn't matter which column you're in.

CAUTION

You can only use this method to delete multiple rows if the rows are next to each other. If there are extra rows between the rows that you want to delete (for example, if you want to delete rows 19, 27, 30, and 33), you cannot use this method.

Press Alt-F7 to go into the Table Editor. Press Delete. The following prompt appears at the bottom of the screen:

    Delete: 1 Rows; 2 Columns: 0

Press R for Rows. You see another prompt:

    Number of Rows: 1

Unless you change the number, WordPerfect only deletes the row with the cursor in it. Type the number of rows you want to delete; then press Enter. They're gone.

CAUTION

Make sure that the rows are either blank or contain text that you don't want. When you delete a row, any text in that row is also deleted.

Press F7 to leave the Table Editor.

▼ If you delete more rows than you bargained for, you can bring them back, but only if you act quickly. You need to be in the Table Editor to bring back deleted rows, so if you've already exited to the document screen, press Alt-F7. Move the cursor so that it's in the row below where the deleted rows ought to go. Press F1. WordPerfect asks whether you want to undelete those rows. Press Y for Yes.

▼ Yes, it's possible to add and remove columns, too. However, it's a real pain in the neck—avoid it at all costs. Make sure you get the right number of columns in your table the first time.

TIP

To remove a single row, move the cursor so that it's in the row you want to remove. Press Ctrl-Delete. WordPerfect asks whether you want to delete the row. Press Y for Yes, and the row is now just a memory.

Using Tables to Emphasize an Existing Paragraph

(Wrap it up, I'll take it)

If you have a certain paragraph in your document that is absolutely positively critically important for your audience to read, you can put a double-lined border around it. How? Use the Block and Tables feature together. Here's what you do:

1. Move the cursor to the beginning of the paragraph that you want to emphasize.

2. If the paragraph begins with a tab, erase the tab.

You can erase a tab by moving your cursor in front of the tab and pressing Delete, or moving the cursor right after the tab and pressing Backspace.

3. Press Alt-F4 to turn on Block.

4. Move the cursor to the end of the paragraph.

Your cursor should be right after the period in the last sentence. The entire paragraph is now highlighted.

5. Press Alt-F7.

This prompt appears at the bottom of the screen:

```
1 Columns; 2 Tables; 3 Math: 0
```

6. Press T for Tables.

Now this prompt appears:

```
Table: 1 Create; 2 Edit: 0
```

You want to create a table around this paragraph, so you'll choose the Create option.

7. Press C for Create.

Yet another prompt appears:

```
Create Table from: 1 Tabular Column;
2 Parallel Column: 0
```

8. Press T for Tabular Column.

Finally, the flurry of prompts ceases, and your paragraph appears, completely roped in by the table-border.

9. Press F7 to leave the Table Editor.

Checklist

▼ If you want a tab at the beginning of your boxed paragraph, move the cursor so that it's under the first letter in the paragraph; then press Home, Tab.

▼ Don't box in more than one paragraph at a time. If you do, there'll be a dividing line between each paragraph.

CHAPTER 19

Speeding Things Up with Macros

(The Not-So-Scary World of Macros)

IN A NUTSHELL

▼ Learn what a macro is

▼ Make macros

▼ Fix a macro you recorded incorrectly

▼ Use macros

▼ Put a signature block in the document

▼ Turn italic on and off

▼ Turn on double line spacing or single line spacing

▼ Turn on page numbering

CHAPTER 19

Macros. The word strikes fear into the heart of almost all WordPerfect users. And why not? *Macro* sounds like something a mad scientist might name his pet robot.

Once you get to know them, though, macros aren't scary at all. In fact, a *macro* is just a shortcut. For example, if you write a lot of letters, you might like to have a shortcut for typing your address or the signature block. This chapter shows you how to make a macro that types up your entire address when you press a single keystroke combination. You also learn about other macro shortcuts that make using WordPerfect easier.

Making and Using Macros

Creating WordPerfect macros is a lot like making audio tapes on a tape recorder. When you want to record something on a tape recorder, you follow certain steps. First, you pop a tape into the machine. Next, you press the Record button. You say what you need to say, and then you turn off the tape recorder.

Later, when you want to play back what you said, you find the tape and put it back in the machine. Then you press Play. You don't have to do anything else—just let the tape recorder do the talking.

WordPerfect macros work the same way. Instead of recording your voice, however, they record and play back things you do in WordPerfect.

To make a macro, you first name the macro with a keystroke combination like Alt-V—this is like popping a tape into the tape recorder and pressing Record. Next, you do the steps you want to be in your macro shortcut. For example, if you want a macro to turn on page numbering, you press the keystrokes to turn on page numbering. Finally, you stop recording the macro.

Later, when you want WordPerfect to do those steps again, you just play the macro by pressing the same keystroke combination you used to name the macro. WordPerfect plays back the macro, doing all those steps for you—very quickly.

Recording a Macro (Record!)

TIP

Before you record a macro shortcut, you should go to a blank document screen. That way, you won't put codes and text you don't want in the document you're using right now.

If you want to automate a task you perform over and over, create a macro. Here's how:

1. Press Ctrl-F10. Ctrl-F10 is the Macro Record key. It tells WordPerfect that you're about to create a shortcut.

This prompt appears at the bottom of the screen:

    Define macro:

What should you name the shortcut? Pick any letter from A-Z.

TIP

Think of a letter that you can associate with the shortcut you're creating. If you want a shortcut for taking you into View Document, use V for View.

2. Hold down the Alt key and press the letter you want to use for this shortcut.

In other words, press and hold down the Alt key. While still holding down that key, press any letter. For example, if you want to use Alt-V as a shortcut to bring up View Document, press Alt-V. Remember this keystroke combo so that you can use your shortcut later.

This prompt appears:

```
Description:
```

3. Type a short description of the macro and press Enter.

`Macro Def` appears in the lower left corner of the screen. You're all set to press the keys you want to be part of your shortcut.

4. Type the text or use the feature you want to be in your shortcut.

For example, if you wanted to make a macro that takes you into the View Document feature and shows you the full page, press Shift-F7, V for View Document; then press 3 for Full Page. As you press your keys, WordPerfect records your actions.

5. Press Ctrl-F10 to stop recording the macro. Then press F7 to return to your document.

You're done.

Checklist

▼ You might want your macro to take you to a certain part of WordPerfect—such as View Document—and leave you there. That's fine. Just begin recording the macro and press the keystrokes you normally would to take you to the menu or screen you want. After you're there, press Ctrl-F10 to tell WordPerfect to stop recording. You can then exit by pressing F7 until you're back at your document screen.

▼ You can type text for your macros or turn features on and off, or any combination of the two. Anything you do often in WordPerfect, you can do faster in a macro.

▼ When you're recording a macro shortcut, don't rush through things! WordPerfect records your mistakes as well as everything else you do. When you're recording a macro, take your time.

▼ When you press Alt and a letter key, you may see a prompt that says the macro already exists. This means you already have a macro by that name. Press F1 to cancel recording the macro (unless you *want* to replace the existing macro); then start over. This time use a different Alt-letter combo.

Redoing the Macro (I goofed up!)

If you get lost or confused while creating a macro, press Ctrl-F10 to quit. Clear your screen, and then start over.

Press Ctrl-F10; then press the Alt-letter combo for the macro to be re-done. This prompt appears:

    your macro name.WPM Already Exists: 1 Replace; 2 Edit;
    3 Description: 0

Press R for Replace. WordPerfect wants to make sure you really mean it, so it asks:

    Replace (*your macro name*)? No (Yes)

Press Y to replace your old macro with the one you're about to record; then type the text or press the keys you want to record. When you are finished, press Ctrl-F10.

Using Your Macro Shortcuts (Play!)

After you create your macro shortcut, all the hard work is done. Now you can save all kinds of time by using the macro shortcut.

Move your cursor to where you want it to be when you play back your macro shortcut. For example, if you're about to use a macro shortcut that starts page numbering in your document, move your cursor to where you want page numbering to begin. Press the Alt-letter keystroke combo you used to name the macro when you created it.

That's it. The macro goes to work, often finishing its task before you can blink.

"I HATE THIS!"

My macro doesn't work on Wallace's machine!

Your macro shortcuts only work on your machine. If you try them on another person's copy of WordPerfect, nothing will happen. You'll have to create the macro on the other machine as you did on your machine.

Macros You Can Use

There are certain WordPerfect tasks most users do over and over again. Here are the steps to create macro shortcuts for some of these common WordPerfect tasks. These are just ideas, though; feel free to experiment and create your own macros.

These steps are pretty bare-bones; they don't detail what the prompts mean or unexpected messages that might pop up. You can learn more about recording and using macros at the beginning of this chapter.

Make a Signature Block Macro

A *signature block* is the last thing you put in your letters. It's the part where you type *Sincerely*, leave space for your signature, and then insert your name and title beneath. This is the easiest type of macro to create. You just start recording the macro, type your signature block the way you always do, and then stop recording the macro.

Here are the steps:

1. Press Ctrl-F10.

2. Press Alt-B.

I chose Alt-B because it reminds me of Signature **B**lock. If you want to use a different Alt-letter keystroke combo, press that combination.

3. Type **SIGNATURE** and press Enter.

4. Press Enter twice.

5. Type **Sincerely,**.

Or, if you prefer, you can type **Thank you,** or **Your Friend,** or **Eat Rocks,** or any other closing you like to use.

6. Press Enter four times.

7. Type your name, press Enter, and then type your title. If you want, you can type your company name under that.

8. Press Ctrl-F10.

This tells WordPerfect to stop recording your macro shortcut.

▼ Whenever you want to put your signature block at the end of a letter, move your cursor so that it's at the end of the last paragraph and press Alt-B. Your signature block appears almost instantaneously.

▼ You can use this same technique to make macro shortcuts for other text you use frequently. For example, you might want to make an Alt-N macro that inserts your name. You could make a Alt-A macro to insert your address. There are probably other words or phrases you use often enough that you could save time by having a macro type them for you.

Turn Italic On and Off

There's a way you can avoid all the finger aerobics necessary for turning on italic. In fact, you'll just have to remember one keystroke combo to turn italic on and off, saving all kinds of time and frustration.

Here are the steps:

1. Press Ctrl-F10.

2. Press Alt-I.

I is for Italic. If you want to use a different Alt-letter keystroke combo, press it.

3. Type **ITALIC** and press Enter.

4. Press Ctrl-F8, A, I.

5. Press Ctrl-F10.

This tells WordPerfect to stop recording your macro shortcut.

▼ The next time you want to use italic, press Alt-I, type your italicized text, and then press Alt-I again to turn off italic.

▼ You can use the Alt-I macro to make existing text italic, too. Move your cursor so that it's under the first character you want italic; then turn on Block by pressing Alt-F4. Move your cursor so that it's after the last character you want to be italic. By now, all the text you want italic should be highlighted. Now, press Alt-I.

Switch between Single and Double Spacing

Certain writing styles require that most of your text is double spaced, except indented quotes, which are supposed to be single spaced. If you need to switch between single and double spacing often, or even if you just use single spacing in some documents and double spacing in others, this pair of macros can save you a lot of wading through WordPerfect's web o' menus.

This is how you make the double spacing macro:

1. Press Ctrl-F10.

2. Press Alt-D.

Alt-D is easy to remember because D stands for **D**ouble. If you want to use a different Alt-letter keystroke combo, press that key combination.

3. Type **DOUBLE SPACE** and press Enter.

4. Press Shift-F8 to bring up the Format menu, L for Line, and then S for Line Spacing.

5. Press 2 for double spacing; then press Enter.

6. Press F7 to return to your document screen.

7. Press Ctrl-F10.

WordPerfect stops recording your macro shortcut.

▼ The steps for creating a macro to turn on single line spacing are almost the same. Follow the steps, except press Alt-S in step 2 (S stands for **S**ingle spacing), and press 1 instead of 2 in step 5.

▼ To use either of these macros, move your cursor to where you want the new line spacing to begin; then press Alt-D for double line spacing, or Alt-S for single line spacing.

Turn On Page Numbering

You need page numbering in just about everything you write, so this is a macro you'll probably use in just about every document. It simply turns page numbering on in the upper right-hand corner. (Or you can make a slight adjustment and make it put the number wherever you want.)

Follow these steps:

1. Press Ctrl-F10.

2. Press Alt-P.

   The P stands for **P**age numbering.

3. Type **PAGE NUMBER** and press Enter.

4. Press Shift-F8 to bring up the Format menu, P for Page, N for Page Numbering, and then P for Position.

5. Press 3 to have page numbers appear in the upper right-hand corner of your pages.

6. Press F7 to return to your document screen.

7. Press Ctrl-F10.

   WordPerfect stops recording your macro shortcut.

Checklist

▼ If you want the page number to go somewhere besides the top left corner of the screen, use a number other than 3 in step 5.

▼ When you want to use this macro, move your cursor so that it's at the top of the page where you want numbering to begin. (An easy way to do this is to press Ctrl-Home, type the page number, and then press Enter.) Press Alt-P to start the macro.

▼ If you don't want your page numbering to start until page 2, move your cursor so it's in the middle of page 1 and press Alt-P.

PART VI

"I Need to Do This NOW!"

Includes:

CHAPTER 20

Create a Memo

(Memo Magic)

IN A NUTSHELL

- ▼ Create an attention-getting heading
- ▼ Add the address
- ▼ Make a divider line
- ▼ Type the memo

Business people seem to have some sort of obsession for memos. They crave writing them and are suspicious of those who don't. One employer I had would often write one memo, then another memo detailing how the previous memo should be filed, and occasionally another memo explaining the reasons he wrote the previous two memos. He was the Memo King.

Even if you aren't memo-happy, you may have to write the occasional memo. And what you have to say is important; it shouldn't be ignored with a bunch of other papers. To catch your audience's eye, you need memos that look professional, open, and inviting. This chapter teaches you the memo magic.

The heading, memo information section, and divider line all contribute to an eye-catching memo.

M E M O R A N D U M

To: Bob Cratchit
From: Ebeneezer Scrooge
Date: December 24, 1992
Subject: The gig's up.

Remember the "vision" I had several years past that changed my life—and your income—so much? Well, surprise, surprise. Evidently they were not real ghosts. Nor were they a dream, prompted by a guilty conscience. They weren't even hallucinations brought on by food poisoning. As you well, know, Bob, they were actors—hired by *you* to trick me into increasing your salary.

Before you come running into my office protesting, you may as well know that I have irrefutable proof. I was rummaging through the cellar last week when I happened on a few old costumes, some chains, and a fog machine. Sure, everything was a little dusty, but still recognizable.

I wanted to believe that you had no part in this chicanery, but DNA tests at the lab helped me make a positive ID on several of the actors, who were quick enough to confirm everything. One of them (the Ghost of Christmas Past, apparently) even mentioned that you and she have stayed in contact. She showed me a working script you've come up with for the stage and said you hope to sell the movie rights for 1.8 million dollars soon. I went through hell, and you want to make a *movie* of it? It seems you could at least have changed my name.

You'll hear from my lawyers soon.

Creating a Heading with Punch

It should be immediately obvious to your readers that they've got a memo in their hands. So, first add all kinds of extra emphasis to the heading: make it all caps, centered, bold, and big. You can also use one other trick to make *Memorandum* extra-prominent: put a space after each letter. This makes the word unusually wide and impossible to miss.

Here's the combination platter for that attention-grabbing header. You can follow all or any of the options you want:

▼ To center the heading, press Shift-F6.

▼ To make the heading bold, press F6.

▼ To make the heading extra large, press Ctrl-F8, S for Size, and then V for Very Large.

After you add the emphasis, type the text. For instance, type **M E M O R A N D U M**. Press the space bar after each letter if you want to make the word extra wide. Then press Enter. Press End to turn off bold and extra large.

TIP

Pressing End moves your cursor to the end of the line, past all the text and text emphasizers.

Creating the Memo's "Address"

Next you add the information that tells who the memo is from, who it's for, and what it is about. First, press Enter three times to add some room between your snazzy header and the address.

The main goal for these lines is accessibility. You want plenty of space between lines.

This is how you make a memo address:

1. Type **To:**, press F4 twice, type who the memo is to, and then press Enter twice.

2. Follow step 1 for the *From*, *Date*, and *Subject* lines.

When you're done, your cursor should be at the beginning of the second line after *Subject*. Now you can create the line that separates this section of the memo from its message.

TIP

Instead of typing the date for the *Date* line, you can insert today's date by pressing Shift-F5, T.

EXPERTS ONLY

Line 'em up

You can make the words To, From, Date, and Subject right-aligned as shown in the example at the beginning of this chapter. To do so, you need to set a right-aligned tab where you want to words to align, and then press Tab *before* you type each word.

Create a Separator Line

The last thing you do before typing the memo's message is create a *separator line*. The separator line's job is simple: it sets the preliminary information apart from the memo's message.

First, press Alt-F9. The following menu appears at the bottom of your screen:

```
1 Figure; 2 Table Box; 3 Text Box; 4 User Box; 5 Line;
6 Equation: 0
```

Press L to create a line. This menu comes up:

```
Create Line: 1 Horizontal; 2 Vertical; Edit Line: 3
Horizontal; 4 Vertical: 0
```

Press H to create the line; then press F7 to return to the document screen. When you press H, a full-sized menu appears, but there's nothing you need to do in it, so you just press F7. You can't see the horizontal line you just created, but it's there, and it will print correctly.

Press Enter twice. This puts some space between the line and where you begin typing your message.

TIP

Before you begin typing the memo, save the framework. Save it with some generic name such as **MEMO**. Then, next time you need to write a memo, you can skip all the steps you just went through. You'll just retrieve the MEMO file and change the To, Date, and Subject lines. Type the text for the memo, and then save the memo with a different name.

Typing the Memo

Now all you have to do is type your suggestions, advice, directions, party plans—whatever you want in the memo.

CHAPTER 21

Write a Letter
(Build a Better Letter)

IN A NUTSHELL

▼ Set up the margins for letterhead
   stationery
▼ Add the date stamp
▼ Add the return address
▼ Add the forwarding
   address
▼ Type the letter
▼ Create the signature
   block

A letter is probably the simplest document you can create in WordPerfect. Basically, you type. And you type. This chapter covers all the typing stuff, plus a few other tidbits on letter writing.

A simple letter writing format.

> December 26, 1992
>
> 2323 Brazil St.
> Apt. 14
> East Lansing, MI 80654
>
> Mr. Santa J. Claus
> Santa's Workshop
> The North Pole
>
> Dear Mr. Claus,
>
> Earlier this month, you and I had a discussion. At that time, you assured me I would receive a certain number of items on December the 25th. I am writing this letter to complain that I did *not* get a Ferrari, a speedboat, a new table saw, a laser printer or even a genuine "Indiana Jones" brand fedora.
>
> To refresh your memory, let me tell you what I *did* get. I got any number of ties (none wearable), three paperback novels (which, oddly enough, I have never heard of, but my wife wanted), a cookbook, a chef's apron, and purple derby.
>
> Mr. Claus, I was good all last year. So my question is this: What gives? What do I have to do to get things I want, and not things my wife wants for me? Is it that you like her better than me?
>
> I anxiously look forward to your reply.
>
> Sincerely,
>
>
> Elden C. Nelson
> Confused, Overgrown Child

Adjusting for Letterhead

If you are going to print the letter on letterhead, the first step is to change the margins. (If you aren't printing on letterhead, skip to the next section.)

When you print on letterhead, you need to start the text of the letter farther down the page. Otherwise, you'll print right on top of the "head" of the letter. To avoid this unsightly problem, change the top margin. Press Shift-F8, P for Page, and then M for Margins. Press 2 and press Enter to set a 2-inch top margin. This size margin works for most letterheads. Press F7 to return to the document.

TIP

If your letter will be shorter than one page, it will look nicer if you center it between the top and bottom margins—like the letter shown in this chapter. To center the letter this way, press Shift-F8, P for Page, C for Center Page, and Y for Yes. Then press F7 to return to your document screen. Your text won't look like it's centered between the top and bottom margins. Don't worry. It is, and it will print correctly.

The Date Stamp

The date is usually the first thing you put in a letter. With WordPerfect, you don't even have to type in the date. Just press Shift-F5, T to put today's date in your document. Now press Enter twice to add some space between the date and your address.

TIP

If you want the date to be up against the right margin, instead of against the left margin, press Alt-F6; then press Shift-F5, T.

275

Return to Sender

The return address is just your address, and nothing could be simpler than typing it. Just type your address, pressing Enter after each line. After you're done with the last line in your address, press Enter twice to make a space between the return address and the *addressee*—the person you're writing.

Checklist

▼ If you're printing the letter on pre-made letterhead, don't include the return address. It's already on the letterhead.

▼ The return address part of the letter usually includes only the address—not your name. Your name will be included in the *signature block*.

▼ A lot of people put the ZIP code on its own line. Don't. Put the ZIP code on the same line as the city and state.

The Forwarding Address

The forwarding address is just the address of the person you're writing. Typing the forwarding address is a cinch. You just type each line of the address, pressing Enter after each line. After you've typed the last line of the address, press Enter twice to put some distance between the address and the beginning of the letter.

The Body of the Letter

(The main attraction)

Writing the letter is just like writing anything in WordPerfect—you just type away. Here are a couple of tricks you should know to get the best possible results:

Checklist

▼ To make the letter opening, type **Dear Mr. Claus,** (or whomever you're writing), and then press Enter twice to make some space between the opening and the body of the letter.

▼ There are a few ways you can begin new paragraphs. If you want a space between each paragraph, press Enter twice at the end of each paragraph. If you *don't* want a blank line between paragraphs, press Enter only once; then press Tab to indent the first line of the new paragraph.

▼ It's okay to open with "Dear Frank," even if Frank isn't dear to you.

The Signature Block

(Your John Hancock)

After you've penned your letter, it's time to assign your John Hancock. First, press Enter twice to put some room between the letter and the signature. Next, type the closing. You can type **Sincerely**, **Warm Wishes**, **God Save the Queen**—whatever your sentiments are at the time.

Then press Enter four times. This makes room for your signature. Type your name. If you need to put a title, press Enter and type it here.

You're all set to send the letter to the printer. When you print your letter, don't just stuff it into an envelope. Remember to sign it!

"I HATE THIS!"

My name won't fit!

One of the most frustrating things that can happen when you're writing a letter is getting to the end of the letter and finding that your signature block isn't going to fit on the current page. You don't want the signature block on a page of its own. What do you do? If you have any extra blank lines, delete them. If you can combine paragraphs, do so. You can also change your margins to allow more lines on the page. Or if you are really, really, really trying to cram something on the page, change the line spacing, as described in Chapter 10.

TIP

If you write a lot of letters, you can speed up creating your address and signature block by using macros. Learn how in Chapter 19.

CHAPTER 22

Create a Form Letter

(Dear Fill-In-the-Blank)

IN A NUTSHELL

- ▼ Create the form letter
- ▼ Make a list of the names and addresses of the recipients
- ▼ Merge the letter and the list

ou need to send the same letter out to lots of people. On one hand, you don't want to send a generic letter. You want to personalize it. On the other hand, you don't want to type the same letter over and over. Is there a solution? Yes! Use WordPerfect's Merge feature.

The idea behind Merge is to write a form letter with some fill-in-the-blank parts, like the recipient's name and address. You then create another document that has a list of the information to fill in those blanks. Then, using the magic of WordPerfect's Merge feature, you combine the two documents, making a personal letter to each person.

This chapter shows you how to work the magic. If you don't need to send form letters, skip this chapter. If you do need to, read on. The process may seem scary, but it's much easier and less painful than typing the same letter to 50 people. After you follow along and see those 50 letters magically appear, you'll thank me for including this chapter.

A Quick Preview

To create a personalized form letter, you need two documents: the primary file and the secondary file. The *primary file* contains the standard text—the text you want to send to everyone. This document also includes secret codes (called *fields*) that tell WordPerfect, "Insert something personal from the secondary file here."

BUZZWORDS

FIELD

A *field* is a special code that you insert into your main document. The field tells WordPerfect where to insert personal text.

The *secondary file* contains all the personal information you want to insert, such as the list of names and addresses that you want to use.

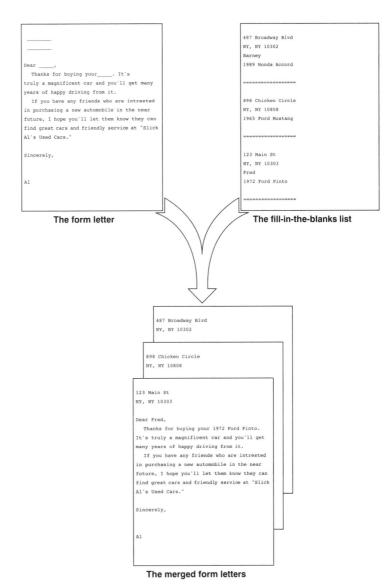

Use Merge to combine a form letter and a list of names, addresses, and other information to create customized form letters.

Creating the First Document

(The Stuff You Want to Say to Everyone)

You create the primary file in about the same way you create any document. Just type away. But here's the key: where you want to insert *personal* information, you insert a field code. You might want the letter to begin *Dear John*. Because the word *Dear* is unchanging text that will be in every letter, just type it.

On the other hand, you don't want *John* in each letter (unless, of course, everyone you're sending the letter to is named John, which isn't likely). Instead, you want WordPerfect to insert a different name for each letter. (Those names will be in the secondary document. More on that later.) To tell WordPerfect to insert a name from a secondary document, you insert a field code instead of typing **John**.

Here's how you insert field codes:

1. Move your cursor to where you want the field.

Common places for fields are the address and the greeting.

2. Press Shift-F9.

A menu appears at the bottom of the screen:

```
1 Field; 2 End Record; 3 Input; 4 Page Off;
5 Next Record; 6 More: 0
```

3. Press F for Field.

WordPerfect shows you this prompt at the bottom of the screen:

```
Enter Field:
```

4. Type a word that describes the kind of information to go into this spot; then press Enter.

Give each field a unique name so that WordPerfect can tell one field from another. Think of a word that describes the kind of information you want to go in this spot, such as *address* or *first name*.

The field appears in your document, looking something like this:

```
{FIELD}first name~
```

{FIELD} always signals the beginning of your field, and the tilde (~) signals the end of it. The text in between is the name of the field.

5. On a piece of paper, write down the name you gave to the field you just created.

Make sure that you copy the field name *exactly*. You'll need this field name later.

6. Follow steps 1 through 5 for each place in the letter where you want custom information. Your primary file looks something like this:

Field code ────

```
June 30, 1993

{FIELD}Address1~
{FIELD}Address2~

Dear {FIELD}Name~,

    Thanks for buying your {FIELD}Car~. It's truly a magnificent car and
you'll get many years of happy driving from it.

    If you have any friends who are interested in purchasing a new
automobile in the near future, I hope you'll let them know they can
find great cars and friendly service at "Slick Al's Used Cars."

Sincerely,

Al


                                          Doc 1 Pg 1 Ln 1" Pos 1"
```

7. When you're finished creating the form letter, save it like you would any document; then clear the screen. Be sure that you remember the name you use to save this primary file!

You need a clean screen to create the fill-in-the-blanks list (the secondary file).

Checklist

▼ You can use a field more than once in a document. For example, you want to use someone's first name several times in a document. Insert a {FIELD}first name~ code in each place you want the first name. Sweepstakes letters often insert the name several times:

> You, **Elden Nelson**, might have won a lot of money. That's right, **Elden Nelson**, you could already be a winner...

▼ A field can hold more than one line of text. For example, you'll probably want the reader's address in your form letter, but your form letter doesn't have to have separate fields for each line of the address. Just insert one field, {FIELD}address~, on a line by itself. The extra lines the address needs will be added when you combine this letter with your fill-in-the-blanks list.

▼ If you want a word to come after a field, make sure that you include a space after the tilde (~) in your field. If you want the field to be the last thing in a sentence, make sure the period comes right after the tilde. And if you want a couple of blank lines after a field (such as the address field) make sure that you press Enter a couple of times after the field.

▼ If you make a mistake adding a field, just use the Delete or Backspace key to delete it or change a name.

CHAPTER 22

Creating the Second Document

(Fill-in-the-blanks)

OK. You've got the letter all set up. Now you have to tell WordPerfect what to insert into the blanks (fields).

There are two parts to making the fill-in-the-blanks list (the secondary file). First, you tell WordPerfect what you've named your fields. Second, you type the information for each person.

Before you begin, make sure that you're at a blank document screen.

Name Your Fields (Field of dreams)

At the beginning of the fill-in-the-blanks list, you need to tell WordPerfect what information you'll be putting into the list. This is WordPerfect's cheat sheet for the fields you inserted. Here's how you do it:

1. Press Shift-F9 twice.

A box of strange, non-English words appears in the upper right corner of the screen. They are called *Advanced Merge Codes* and are corrosive, explosive, and highly toxic. Fortunately, you won't have to do much in this box.

2. Press F, down-arrow key.

This is now highlighted in the window:

    {FIELD NAMES}name1~...nameN~~

285

3. Press Enter.

This prompt appears at the bottom of the screen:

```
Enter Field 1:
```

4. Type the field names you wrote down, pressing Enter after each one. You don't have to type any of the special characters like the tilde or the brackets. Just type the name. For instance, if you have a field named *address*, just type **address**.

Type the field names in the order that you will enter the fields. For example, if you'll type the first name, last name, address, and phone number, type the field names in that same order.

5. When you're finished typing the field names, press Enter.

The prompt disappears, and something like the following mess appears at the top of your screen:

```
(FIELD NAMES)Address1~Address2~Name~Car~~ (END RECORD)
==============================================================================




                                           Doc 1 Pg 1 Ln 1" Pos 1"
```

The {FIELD NAMES} code tells Word-Perfect what information you'll put in your fill-in-the-blanks list.

▼ Notice that each of your field names is followed with a tilde (~).

▼ The last field name has two tildes after it, which tells WordPerfect that you're all finished with your field names.

▼ The field names end with an {END RECORD} code and a page break that looks like a double-dashed row across your screen.

▼ Don't delete any of the tildes or codes in the field names section of your list. You can, however, edit the text of the field names, if you need to. Just make sure that each field name ends with a tilde, and that the last one has two tildes after it.

Make the Fill-in-the-Blanks List

The ugly part is over. Now you simply type the information for each letter. (You should still be in the document with the field code cheat sheet at the top.)

1. Type the text for the current field.

If you're not sure what field you're in, look at the bottom left corner of the screen. The field name appears there.

CAUTION

Don't press Enter after you type the text, unless you're typing a multi-line field like an address. If you do accidentally press Enter, press Backspace to go back up to the previous line.

Also, if you are typing a multi-line field, press Enter at the end of each line—except the last one.

2. After you type the field, press F9.

This puts an {END FIELD} code at the cursor and takes you down to the next line. The {END FIELD} code just tells WordPerfect that you're finished entering one piece of information for one person and are ready to enter another piece of information.

"I HATE THIS!"

Do I really need those codes?

This step is very important! If you forget to press F9 and put in an {END FIELD} code, WordPerfect gets all out of whack and is prone to mistake one field for another. Even if you don't have anything to type for a certain field, press F9 to insert the {END FIELD} code on a line by itself.

3. Repeat steps 1 and 2 for each field in the letter.

After you've typed all the fill-in-the-blank information about one person, you're ready to start over, typing the same kind of information about the next person who will receive the letter. Before you can do that, though, you need to signal to WordPerfect that you're finished with the custom information for one letter, and are ready to begin again.

4. Press Shift-F9, E.

This puts an {END RECORD} code on a line by itself, and then a page break (which looks like a line of equal signs across the screen). Notice that the prompt at the bottom of the screen is asking for the first field again.

5. Repeat steps 1-4 until you've typed the fill-in-the-blank information for each form letter.

6. Save the document, and then clear the screen. Be sure to save the document with a name that you remember.

The document that you just created is the secondary file, and it looks something like this:

End Field code ⟶

End Record code ⟶

```
{FIELD NAMES}Address1~Address2~Name~Car~~{END RECORD}
----------------------------------------------------------------
487 Broadway Blvd{END FIELD}
New York, NY 10302{END FIELD}
Barney{END FIELD}
1989 Honda Accord{END RECORD}
----------------------------------------------------------------
B98 Chicken Circle{END FIELD}
New York, NY 10800{END FIELD}
Ken{END FIELD}
1965 Ford Mustang{END RECORD}
----------------------------------------------------------------
123 Main St{END FIELD}
New York, NY 10303{END FIELD}
Fred{END FIELD}
1972 Ford Pinto{END RECORD}
----------------------------------------------------------------



                                        Doc 1 Pg 1 Ln 1" Pos 1"
```

BUZZWORDS

RECORD

The custom information for one letter is called a record. That's why the code at the end of each series of fields is called {END RECORD}.

Merging the Two Letters

(All Together Now)

Okay. So you've made your form letter and your fill-in-the-blanks list. Now you're ready to combine the two into your personalized, customized, gee-whiz, merged letters.

Make sure that you're at a blank document screen. Then follow these steps:

1. Press Ctrl-F9.

This prompt appears:

```
1 Merge; 2 Sort; 3 Convert Old Merge Codes: 0
```

2. Press M for Merge.

This prompt appears at the bottom of your screen:

```
Primary file:
```

WordPerfect wants to know the name of your form letter file.

3. Type the name of your form letter; then press Enter.

For example, if you were making a form letter to clients who hadn't paid up, you might have named your form letter DEADBEAT. In that case, you would type **DEADBEAT** here; then press Enter.

The following prompt appears:

```
Secondary file:
```

Now WordPerfect wants to know the name of your fill-in-the-blanks list.

4. Type your fill-in-the-blanks list file name; then press Enter.

`* Merging *` appears in the lower left corner of your screen, letting you know that WordPerfect is busy combining your two files.

When the merge is done, all of your personalized form letters are in one document, with page breaks (rows of equal signs) separating each letter.

Checklist

▼ If you've got an especially large fill-in-the-blanks list, the merge could take a while.

▼ The document created by your merge doesn't have a name. If you want to keep the document, you need to save it.

▼ You can print your merged file right from the document screen. Just press Shift-F7, F. Make sure you've got plenty of paper in the printer!

TOMORROW IS THE START OF A WHOLE NEW WEEK.

I BETTER GET MY EXCUSES ORGANIZED.

WELL, NO, I DIDN'T GET TO IT BECAUSE THE COPIER WENT DOWN YESTERDAY.

NOPE. DIDN'T GET THE MESSAGE... THERE'S SOMETHING WRONG WITH MY MACHINE.

SORRY... I MEANT TO GET IT TO YOU YESTERDAY...

BUT MY FAX IS ON THE BLINK.

I TRIED TO CALL IN FROM THE ROAD, BUT MY CAR PHONE'S IN THE SHOP.

I WOULD HAVE FINISHED IT YESTERDAY, BUT THE COMPUTER WENT DOWN...

WELL, THIS MORNING THE LASER PRINTER CRASHED,...

AND I COULDN'T GET MY MODEM ON LINE.

THAT'S THE GREATEST THING ABOUT ALL THIS HIGH-TECH EQUIPMENT:

HIGH-TECH EXCUSES.

PART VII

The Quick and Dirty Dozens

Includes:

Quick and Dirty Dozens

12 Cool Things You Can Do in WordPerfect

1. Get back, Jack.

When you're really on a word processing roll, it's easy to accidentally hit the Page Down key when you meant to simply hit Delete. Now you have to find where you were, right? Wrong. Just press Ctrl-Home twice, and your cursor jumps back to where you were typing. Just make sure you press Ctrl-Home, Ctrl-Home before you do anything else, or WordPerfect will forget where you were last working.

You can use Ctrl-Home for other shortcuts, too. If you want to jump to a certain page, press Ctrl-Home, type the page number where you want to go, and then press Enter. You're there.

2. I've got your number.

You may need to insert the current page number somewhere in your text. *Don't* just type the number you see by Pg in the lower right corner of the screen. After all, that number might change when you edit. Instead, press Ctrl-B. That puts a ^B at your cursor, which doesn't look so hot. However, when you print your document, WordPerfect replaces ^B with the current page number.

Use this ^B trick in headers and footers for page numbers, too.

3. Thinking inside the box.

If you want to call attention to a paragraph, put it in a box. The easiest way of doing this is to create a one-cell table, and then type the text in it. Creating tables is usually a pain in the neck, but this

is an exception. Move your cursor to where you want the paragraph; then press Alt-F7, T, C, 1, Enter, Enter, F7. You've got your box. Now enter your text. You can make it more than one paragraph, but it all needs to fit on one page. After you've got the box the way you want it, press the down-arrow key until you're outside of the box.

4. **You can say that again.**

When you're working on certain topics, chances are you'll use certain words and phrases over and over. No point in retyping them. Use the Alt-number shortcut instead.

First, type the word or phrase you need to use frequently. Press Alt-F4 and use the arrow keys to highlight the text. Then press Ctrl-Page Up. Something appears at the bottom of the screen, like this:

```
Variable:
```

Press a number, 0-9, and then press Enter. Whenever you need that word or phrase, hold down the Alt key and press that number. With no more effort on your part, the text appears. You can use this trick for up to 10 Alt-number combinations. Note that when you leave WordPerfect, the shortcuts are erased.

5. **Where, oh where, has my function key strip gone?**

That strip of paper that goes over your function keys can be a real lifesaver—it shows what finger gymnastics are necessary for you to use WordPerfect's features. Those strips are pretty easy to lose, though. If you can't find your function key strip, press F3 twice to see an on-screen version of the strip. When you're finished looking at the strip, press the space bar to go back to your document.

6. **Find your file fast!**

Instead of pressing F5, Enter to go to List Files, press F5 twice to get there even faster. As an extra bonus, this trick takes you back to the same directory and file you used the last time you were in List Files. This trick is great when you've had to navigate through tons of directories to find a file, and then later find you need to go back to that directory. F5, F5 gets you there without all the finger work.

7. **Joined at the hip.**

It doesn't work to have dates or proper names split across two lines by WordPerfect. You can avoid this problem by pressing Home, space bar (instead of just the space bar) between words that need to be kept on the same line. For instance, if I were Peter Frampton and I were typing my name, I would type Peter, press Home, space bar, and *then* type Frampton. That way, both my first and last name would stay on the same line.

8. **Does anybody really know what time it is?**

One of the most important questions in the world is "How long 'til 5:00?" You can use WP to quickly find the current time by pressing F5, F5 and looking in the upper left corner, which shows the current time, date, and temperature. Okay, the temperature isn't really displayed. Press F7 to go back to the document.

9. **Stuck in the middle with you.**

As you type, your cursor works toward the bottom of the screen until you're stuck at the bottom row, where lines wrap up one at a time. What a nuisance. Press Alt-F3, Alt-F3 and half the screen scrolls up so that your cursor is in the middle of the screen. Go ahead and type until you're at the bottom of the screen, and then do the trick again.

10. **Dashing Dashes.**

An em-dash is, simply enough, a dash about the width of an "m." People use them when they're not sure what punctuation they *really* should be using. You'll notice them in this book—right here, for instance. When using typewriters, people would fake em-dashes by pressing the dash key (-) twice. Now that we've got computers, you can use *real* em-dashes, which look better. Just press Ctrl-2 (not Ctrl-F2) and press the dash (-) key twice.

11. **Printing in the fast lane.**

You may be able to print faster than you think. If the printer you use isn't in a different room from your computer, use this tip to make your print jobs faster. Press Shift-F7, S, E, H, Y, F7, F7, F7. That's a lot of keys to press, but you only have to do it once. I won't even bother to explain why it makes your printing faster. It just does.

12. **Dye your computer.**

If you're using a laptop computer, you may have a tough time seeing text in the View Document feature. You can change the way it looks by pressing Shift-F7, V, Shift-F3. That reverses the colors used in View Document. If you don't like the change, press Shift-F3 again. If you press and hold down Shift-F3, you'll get a disco effect until you release the keys.

After you're happy with colors, press F7 to return to your document screen. The View Document color change will remain in effect until you change it again.

12 Things You Should Never Do in WordPerfect

1. No spaces!

Don't use the space bar to indent the beginning of a paragraph or to make columns.

The space bar is a tempting key—it's so much bigger than all the others. You may be in the habit of pressing the space bar five times each time you start a new paragraph, or using the space bar to line up columns of information. Get out of the habit quickly. If you use the space bar to begin paragraphs or start columns, things may look lined up on-screen, but they probably won't line up on the printed page.

Use the Tab key instead. The Tab key was made specifically for beginning paragraphs and lining up columns.

2. I said, No spaces!

Don't use the space bar to go to the next line in a document. When you need to put some space between paragraphs or lines in a document, don't lean on the space bar until you've created those lines of space. If you ever edit your work, those spaces will shift around and wreak havoc on your document. Instead, when you need to move down a line, just press Enter. If you need to move down a few lines, press Enter a few times. Don't, however, use Enter to go all the way to the next page (that's the next tip).

3. Breaking up is easy to do.

Don't use the Enter key to go to the next page. If you've just finished a title page and want to begin on a fresh page for the body of your document, don't keep pressing Enter until you see that row of dotted lines. Instead, just press Ctrl-Enter.

4. **Save and sort.**

Don't sort a list before you save it. The Sort feature is handy for alphabetizing lists of people, inventories, or whatever. However, it's a tricky process and can sometimes go wrong—and the F1 key can't undo your sort. Before you ever start blocking your list and sorting it, save your document. That way, if things go awry, you can clear the document without saving, retrieve the copy of the file you made before sorting, and then try again.

5. **Save and spell.**

Don't check the spelling of a document before you save it. I used to work in WordPerfect Customer Support, and received dozens of terrified calls from people who had just started WordPerfect's Speller feature...and now the computer had frozen. They hadn't saved their documents yet, and were wondering what could be done to get their work back. The answer is: nothing. For some reason, some copies of WordPerfect occasionally freeze up when you check the spelling of certain documents.

This may never happen to you, but it's better to be safe than sorry. The last thing you should do before starting a spelling check is to save that document. That way, if your computer locks up while you're checking spelling, you can just reset the computer, retrieve the document, and restart the spelling check.

6. **Replacement files.**

Don't blindly replace one file with another. You've been typing away at a new document, and it's time to give it a name. You press F10, type a name, and then press Enter. WordPerfect asks:

```
Replace (your file)? No (Yes)
```

If you aren't intentionally replacing an old file with this new one, press N for No; then type a new name for your new file. Otherwise, you could be erasing a file that you'll need someday.

7. **Proper page number etiquette.**

With typewriters, you had to type page numbers on each page. If you try the same thing in WordPerfect, you'll get disastrous results. Any time you edit the document, your manually typed page numbers will shift around, winding up too far down on the page, or even somehow jumping onto the previous page.

Instead of typing page numbers, use the page numbering feature. Go to the top of the document (press Home, Home, up-arrow key), press Shift-F8, P for Page, N for Page Numbering, P for Page Number Position, and then 3 to have page numbers in the top right corner of the page. Press F7 to return to the document screen. You won't be able to see the page numbers, but they'll be added when you print.

8. **I *probably* don't need this file.**

Don't delete files you don't understand. When you look in your WordPerfect directory (usually C:\WP51), you notice a lot of files. If you're ever in the mood to clear up some space on your hard drive, you may be tempted to delete some of those files. Well, look elsewhere, my friend. Most of those files are critical to WordPerfect running smoothly. Be especially careful not to delete any files that end with .EXE, .COM, .FIL, .PRS, .ALL, .VRS, .DRS, or .FRS.

9. **Security clearance.**

Don't use the Password Protect feature. I didn't cover the Password Protect feature in this book on purpose because it's too tempting. The thought of having your own secret, private files that nobody

but you can read is just too mysterious to resist. You'll probably eventually find the Password feature on your own and want to try it out. Well, the fact is that somebody who's serious about reading your files can get right past your Password; there are a couple of commercially available programs designed to do just that. The chances of you forgetting your password (so you can't retrieve your own file) are much greater than the chances of somebody else wanting to read your diary.

10. **Mystery files.**

Don't use F10 to save your CONFIG.SYS or AUTOEXEC.BAT files. CONFIG.SYS and AUTOEXEC.BAT are files your computer uses every time you turn on the thing. From time to time, you may need to make changes to these files, and WordPerfect's a good program to make those changes.

You can retrieve these files just like you would any document. However, when you're finished making the changes, don't use the F10 key to save these files. That would make them WordPerfect documents, and your computer wouldn't be able to use them to start up. Instead, press Ctrl-F5, T for DOS Text, S for Save.

At the `Document to be saved (DOS Text):` prompt, press Enter. You're asked whether you want to replace the file. Press Y for Yes. This brings you back to the document screen. Press F7, N, N to clear the document from the screen, since you've already saved your changes.

11. **Save, save, save, and save again.**

Don't type a document without frequently saving it. When your typing is really on a roll, it's easy to forget to update your document from time to time. That's a big mistake. You wouldn't like it if all

those brilliant paragraphs were to suddenly go to the great computer graveyard in the sky. But it could happen unless you save your documents early, and save them often. Read Chapter 3, "Save Your Work," to learn how to save and update your documents.

12. **Exit stage right.**

Don't turn off your computer without exiting WordPerfect first. When the whistle blows, you want to turn off the computer and get out of the office as fast as you can. It's almost enough to make you want to just turn off your computer before you exit WordPerfect. Don't do it.

When you exit WordPerfect, it does some important file housecleaning. If you turn off your computer before you exit WordPerfect, the next time you try to use it, WordPerfect will ask you all kinds of strange and time-consuming questions before you can get to work.

12 Heart-Stopping WordPerfect Messages and What to Do about Them

1. `Are other copies of WordPerfect currently running? (Y/N)`

This prompt appears at the bottom of the screen every once in a while when you start WordPerfect. Of course you're not using more than one copy of WordPerfect at a time—you're no glutton for punishment. When you see this message, press N for No. Next, another bizarre prompt might appear:

```
Old document 1 backup file exists. 1 Rename;
2 Delete: 1
```

Press R for rename, type a file name, such as **BACKUP**, and then press Enter. Now you can get back to work in WordPerfect.

Why does this message come up? The last time you used WordPerfect, you didn't exit normally. Either the computer hung up, the power went out, or you just turned off the machine before exiting WordPerfect. So, the next time you start WordPerfect, WordPerfect wants to know if anything is amiss. The file you re-named was the file you were working on last when you shut off the computer. You can retrieve it by pressing Shift-F10, typing **C:\WP51** and the file name you just typed a moment ago, and then pressing Enter.

2. `ERROR: File not found`

This message appears when you try to retrieve a document by pressing Shift-F10, typing a file name, and pressing Enter. The message means that you made a mistake when typing the file name. The message only appears for a moment, then disappears, leaving you at

the `Document to be retrieved:` prompt. Look carefully at the file name you typed. If you see the mistake, correct it, and then press Enter. If you get the message again, press F5, Enter to go to List Files. Then retrieve the document from List Files.

3. `Document not formatted for current printer. Continue?` `No (Yes)`

You get this message every so often when you try to print a document. The message means that when the document was created, a different printer was in use. Go ahead and press Y to have the document printed.

You'll usually get this message when you try to print a document that somebody else created and then gave to you on a floppy disk.

4. `ERROR: Incompatible file format`

This message just means that you've tried to retrieve a file that WordPerfect can't read. For example, you'll get this message if you try to retrieve a program, a graphic file, or another word processor file. This message appears, lets you read it for a moment, and then disappears.

Don't bother trying to retrieve the file again, you won't have any better luck the second time. If you're in List Files when you get this message, you probably accidentally highlighted the wrong file. Highlight the right one and try retrieving again.

5. `ERROR: Invalid file name`

You get this error when you try to save a file using characters that DOS can't use. The following characters are the biggest culprits:

> ? . *

Type a different name without those characters.

6. `Cancel all print jobs? No (Yes)`

You've sent one or more print jobs to the printer, and now you want to leave WordPerfect. Problem is, WordPerfect's not done printing. If you really have decided that you don't want to print after all, press Y to cancel all your print jobs and leave WordPerfect. Otherwise, press N to return to the WordPerfect screen.

7. `ERROR: Access denied`

This nasty-sounding message reads like you've just tried to break into NASA's main computer. Nothing so glamorous here. Instead, this message probably means one of three things. It could be that you tried to save a document with a name that already exists and has been protected against being overwritten. Or, you might have tried to give a document the same name as a directory. Finally, the disk you're trying to save to might be full. Try saving with a different name. If that doesn't work, you may need to delete some other documents from your hard disk before you can save this one.

8. `Replace (filename)? No (Yes)`

You've just tried naming a document with the same name as a file that already exists. If you're just updating a document, this is no big deal. Just press Y and get back to work. If you're doing a first save on your document, however, you might be about to erase a file you don't want to lose. Press N, type a different file name, and then press Enter again to save the document with the different file name.

307

9. `Delete [code]? No (Yes)`

You're backspacing or erasing text in your document, when all of a sudden, a strange `Delete [some code goes here]? No (Yes)` prompt appears. This means that you've got some special formatting code at your cursor, and WordPerfect wants to know whether you want to get rid of it. Look at the text between the brackets. If you don't understand it, stay on the safe side and don't delete it—press N for no. If you *do* understand the code, such as [bold] or [underline], and you *do* want to get rid of the formatting for that part of the text, press Y for Yes.

10. `Write protect error writing drive A. Press any key to continue.`

The disk you're trying to save a file on has been fixed so that you can only retrieve information from it, not put new files on it. The best solution is to take the floppy disk out of the drive and use a different floppy disk. Whoever doesn't want you putting files on that disk probably has a pretty good reason.

If you must put a file on that floppy disk, first take it out of the drive. If it's a 5.25-inch disk, there's probably a piece of tape covering up a notch on the right edge of the disk (that is, the right side when you're reading the disk label). Remove that piece of tape, insert the disk into the floppy drive, press a key to make the `Write protect error` message disappear, and then try saving to the floppy disk again.

If you were trying to save to a 3.5-inch disk, remove the disk from the drive, turn it over, and slide the little plastic square (in the upper left corner of the disk) so you can't see a hole through that corner. Put the disk back into the floppy disk drive, press a key to make the `Write protect error` message disappear, and then try saving to the floppy disk again.

11. `Device not ready reading drive A. 1 Retry; 2 Cancel`

You're trying to save a document to your floppy drive, but there's no floppy diskette in there, or the drive door isn't closed. Make sure you've got a disk in the drive, close the door, and press 1 to try saving again.

12. `ERROR: Invalid drive/path specification`

You're trying to save or retrieve a file to a certain directory, but that directory doesn't exist. This almost always means that you typed the name of the directory wrong. This message only appears for a moment, and then it disappears of its own accord. Take a look at the directory the way you typed it, fix whatever you mistyped, and press Enter to try again.

12 Features You Should Leave Alone Unless You Have Time to Kill

1. Advanced Advance.

You can make your cursor magically move to any point on the page by using the Advance command. This is nice if you need to put a word exactly 2.75 inches from the top of the page or 1.89 inches from the left side of the page. If you need WordPerfect to print on pre-printed forms, you may need to deal with Advance.

Press Shift-F8, 4 for Other, and then A for Advance. The following menu appears at the bottom of the screen:

```
Advance: 1 Up; 2 Down; 3 Line; 4 Left; 5 Right;
6 Position: 0
```

Press I for Line if you want to specify how far from the top of the page (not margin) you want your text to be, or press P for Position to tell WordPerfect how far from the left side of the page you want the text to be. Type the measurement you want; then press Enter. Press F7 to return to the document screen.

2. Where's the end of the paragraph?

When you're using WordPerfect, it's sometimes handy to know where you've pressed Enter. If you want a symbol to appear on-screen at the end of paragraphs, press Shift-F1, D for Display, E for Edit-Screen Options, H for Hard Return Display Character. Here's where you can type the character you want to show up whenever you press Enter. I recommend the paragraph symbol (¶). To insert this, press Ctrl-2 (not Ctrl-F2); then type **4,5** (don't forget the comma between the 4 and 5) and press Enter. You won't see

anything happen until you press Enter. Press F7 to return to your document screen. Now, when you press Enter at a document screen, the end of your paragraph is signaled by a paragraph symbol. This symbol only shows up on-screen, not on the printed page.

If you decide you don't like having an end-of-paragraph marker after all, press Shift-F1, D for Display, E for Edit-Screen Options, H for Hard Return Display Character. Then press the space bar to get rid of the character. Press F7 to return to your document screen.

3. **The menu thing.**

One of WordPerfect's best-kept secrets is that it works pretty well with a mouse. If you like using a mouse with other programs, you might give it a shot with WordPerfect. To see WordPerfect's mouse menu bar, click the right button on the mouse. You can then select menus and features like you would in any of your Windows programs. The mouse menu disappears when you've selected something, or you can make it disappear by clicking either mouse button outside the menu bar.

4. **Overstrike! Overstrike!**

Some day, a crazy notion to print two characters on top of each other may come into your head. For instance, you may want a zero with a slash through it (∅) to make sure that nobody mistakes it for a capital O. The Overstrike feature lets you put two characters on top of each other. Press Shift-F8, 4 for Other, O for Overstrike, C for Create. Then type the two characters you want printed on top of each other. Press Enter, F7 to return to your document screen. On the WordPerfect screen, only the second character in the overstrike will appear, but they both will appear—on top of each other—on the printed page.

5. **Outlines made easy.**

Outlines are nice when you've got to make an agenda for a meeting
or an outline for a book or report. WordPerfect's Outline feature
puts an adjustable outline level on-screen whenever you press
Enter.

To turn on Outline, press Shift-F5, O for Outline, O for On. Press
Enter to get your first outline number. Press F4 so that all your
outline text will be indented at the same level; then type your text
for that level. Press Enter to go to the next outline item.

If you want to move down an outline level, press Tab. If you want
to move up a level, press Shift-Tab. Each time you press Enter,
WordPerfect goes to the previous outline level.

6. **Initial codes unlimited.**

If you use certain margins or line settings all the time in Word-
Perfect, you can set them to be the defaults. Press Shift-F1, I for
Initial Settings, C for Initial Codes. This brings you into a screen
similar to a regular editing screen. Set the margins, justification,
line spacing and whatever other formatting you want in each document as you normally would. Press F7 twice to return to your
document screen. The settings you just made will apply to all
the documents you create from now on.

7. **Etch-A-Sketch.**

This is a silly little feature you might play with when you feel like
doodling. Make sure you're at a blank screen before doing this.
Press Ctrl-F3, and then press L for Line Draw. Now, when you
press your arrow keys, you make a line. Guess what—WordPerfect
has just become an Etch-A-Sketch. You can change to a double

line by pressing 2. When you're finished with this nonsense, press F7 to leave Line Draw, and be sure to clear the screen before your boss comes in and screams at you to quit fiddling around.

8. **Talking to yourself.**

If you want to make a remark to yourself in a document, but don't want that remark to print, try out the Comments feature. Move the cursor to where you want the comment to appear. Then press Ctrl-F5, C for Comment, C for Create. The cursor appears in a box, where you can type away. Press F7 when you're done. Your comment appears in a box on-screen, but it won't print.

9. **Dates your way!**

Usually, WordPerfect's automatic date feature puts the date in this format: February 3, 1993. If you would prefer something different (such as 02/03/93), you can customize the date. Press Shift-F5, and then press F for Date Format. The Date Format menu appears, where you can type any of the examples listed in the screen to get a different format. Press Enter when you're done. Then press T to insert your date into the document.

10. **Happy hyphenation.**

WordPerfect ordinarily keeps entire words together on a line, but you can have it hyphenate automatically as you write. This is most useful if your documents are full-justified. Move the cursor to where you want WordPerfect to begin hyphenating words. Then press Shift-F8, L for Line, Y for Hyphenate, Y for Yes. Then press F7 to return to the document screen.

11. **Redecorating WordPerfect.**

What?! You don't like white-on-blue for writing? You can change your WordPerfect screen colors to black-on-white or whatever else you want. Press Shift-F1, D for Display, C for Colors/Fonts/Attributes. When you come to Setup: Colors/Fonts, press S for Screen Colors.

You are now at the Setup: Colors screen. By changing the letters under Foreground and Background, you're changing the way WordPerfect will look. After you come up with something you like, press F7 twice to return to your document screen.

12. **Two, two, two documents at once.**

WordPerfect's really like having two typewriters at once—you can work on two documents at the same time. Just press Shift-F3 to move from one document to another. Each document works exactly the same. You will, however, have to go through the Exit process twice before you can exit WordPerfect.

12 Common Mistakes

1. I can't get out of Help!

I haven't talked about WordPerfect's Help feature much in this
book. That's because I think it's usually not all that helpful. If you
want to get help, press F3. After looking around for a while, you'll
want out. Your instinct will be to press F7—after all, that's the key
that gets you out of most features. But not Help. If you want to get
out of the Help feature, press Enter or the space bar.

2. I pressed Enter to retrieve a document, but I can't edit it.

In most programs' file managers, you highlight the file you want to
use, and then press Enter to retrieve it. Not so with WordPerfect.
In List Files, pressing Enter activates the Look feature, which lets
you preview a document, but not edit it. If you're fruitlessly trying
to type in your document screen, chances are you automatically
pressed Enter instead of R for Retrieve. Press F7 to leave the Look
feature, and then press R to retrieve the document.

3. Oops! I forgot to turn on my printer.

It doesn't matter how long you've worked with computers, you'll
still occasionally do this one. You send a print job to your printer,
but haven't bothered to turn on the printer. If you turn on the
thing now, your backlogged print jobs should start rolling out in
just a couple of minutes.

4. How do I start a search?

It seems that you activate almost every process in WordPerfect by
pressing Enter. Well, that's not the way it is when you begin a
search. When you want to look for certain text in your document,

press F2 to bring up the `-> Srch:` prompt, type the text you're looking for, and then resist the urge to press Enter. Instead, press F2 again to begin the search.

5. **Bold and italic are running amuck in my document!**

You want to turn on bold for a word, so you press F6 and begin typing. Later, when you print the document, you discover that the rest of the document after that point is bold. The problem is that you forgot to turn *off* bold.

What to do? Move your cursor to where you want bold to stop and press Ctrl-F8, N for Normal. The same goes for italic.

6. **My page doesn't look right.**

It's important to have your cursor in the correct place when you use certain features. If your top and bottom margins or page numbering setups aren't taking effect until the page after you wanted them, make sure that your cursor is at the very top of the page when you set those codes. You can go to the top of the document by pressing Home, Home, up-arrow key. Or you can go to the top of any page by pressing Ctrl-Home, typing the page you want to go to the top of, and then pressing Enter.

7. **Non-System disk? What?**

You're starting a new day of work. You turn on your computer, only to get this message:

```
Non-System disk or disk error
Replace and strike any key when ready
```

The cause of this problem is easy: you have a floppy disk in your A drive. Remove the floppy disk, press the space bar, and get back to work.

I HATE WORDPERFECT!

8. mY tEXT lOOKS wEIRD.

If you're transcribing from something printed, you may not notice accidentally pressing your Caps Lock key when you meant to hit Shift. Now all the characters that you want uppercase are lowercase, and vice versa. You don't have to retype the mess, however. Just move your cursor to the first character where things started being backward. Turn on Block by pressing Alt-F4, and then move the cursor just after the last character you need fixed. Now press Shift-F3, L for Lowercase. This makes everything lowercase except the beginning of sentences. You might need to go and fix proper names, but that's easier than retyping the whole mess.

9. Backspace vs. Delete

Pressing Backspace erases the character to the *left* of your cursor. Pressing Delete erases the character that cursor is *under*. It's that simple, but it's hard to remember. If you've erased in the wrong direction, press F1, R right away to restore the lost text.

10. Did I say Tab? I meant Indent.

If you need a paragraph further to the right than the surrounding text, it's tempting to press Tab at the beginning of each line. Don't. When you edit the paragraph, the tabs will no longer always be at the beginning of each line, and the paragraph becomes a shambles. Instead, right at the beginning of the paragraph, press F4. The entire paragraph is now indented over one tab stop.

11. I inserted my *own* hyphen.

If you're at the end of a line and are about to type a long word (such as *terpsichorean*), you might want to break it up with a hyphen. That way the whole word doesn't wrap to the next line,

317

leaving the previous line looking short. Most people hyphenate the word by moving to the point they want to break the word, pressing the hyphen key (-), and then pressing the space bar.

If you edit the paragraph so that the whole word fits on a single line, you now have something that looks like *terpsi-chorean*. Instead, when you want to hyphenate a word, move to where you want the word to break, then press Ctrl-hyphen to insert the hyphen. If you later edit the paragraph so that the whole word fits on a line, the hyphen automatically disappears.

12. **Numbers mysteriously appear in my document.**

Whenever you first start WordPerfect, the Num Lock key is on automatically. If you're used to using the numeric keypad for cursor movement, that can pose a real problem. If you want to go to the top of the document and press what you think is Home, Home, up-arrow key, you've actually just typed **778** because the keys are acting as numbers.

There are a couple of ways to remedy this problem. First, make a habit of pressing the Num Lock key to turn it off as soon as you start WordPerfect. Second, if your keyboard has a separate keypad for cursor movement, make a habit of using those keys instead of the ones that double as a numeric keypad.

12 Best WordPerfect Shortcuts

Something most people don't know is that WordPerfect comes with a whole slew of useful shortcuts, each of which can be started with by pressing a keystroke combo. But there's a catch. In order to use these shortcuts, you have to tell WordPerfect to use a different keyboard layout—make the keys do different things. Here's how:

1. Press Shift-F1, K for Keyboard Layout.

A list of keyboards appears. The list includes one named Macros.

2. Use the arrow keys to highlight Macros.

3. Press S for Select.

The Setup menu appears, with MACROS.WPK to the right of 5 - Keyboard Layout.

4. Press F7 to return to the document screen.

Now you can use the shortcuts in this quick and dirty dozen.

Return to the Main Editing Screen (Press Alt-E)

Getting in and out of WordPerfect menus is such a chore. You can at least speed up the process of getting out of those menus—and back to your document screen—by using this shortcut. After you've finished making changes in a menu, just press Alt-E to zip back to your document screen, without the usual hassle of having to press F7 several times.

Flip Two Characters (Alt-T)

When you're typing at warp speed, sometimes one hand gets ahead of the other and you type **teh** instead of **the**, or **tihs** instead of **this**. When you make this mistake, instead of backspacing over both the characters, just move the cursor to the right of the mixed up characters and press Alt-T. WordPerfect switches them back into place.

Delete an Entire Line (Alt-D)

If you need to get rid of a line of text—or several lines of text—quickly, move the cursor anywhere on the line to be erased; then press Alt-D. The old line disappears and the one below it jumps up to take its place. You can continue pressing Alt-D to get rid of more lines.

Send the Printer a "Go" (Alt-G)

When you're printing envelopes, WordPerfect usually stops and requires you to go into the Control Printer and tell the printer to start. Instead, press Alt-G from your document screen, which does the same thing without making you chase through the maze o' menus.

Capitalize the First Letter of the Current Word (Alt-C)

I don't need to tell you why this one's useful. If you forget to capitalize a word, you've got to go back, delete the old letter and retype the capital version. Save the effort by moving your cursor anywhere within the word and pressing Alt-C. WordPerfect capitalizes the first letter of the word for you.

Start a Letter, Memo, or Itinerary (Ctrl-D)

I wonder how many millions of memos have been made with Word-Perfect. Or how many legions of letters. A staggering number, no doubt, and I'll bet that you need to add to that count. You can speed up the process with the Ctrl-D shortcut. From a blank document screen, press Ctrl-D. You see the prompt, `Enter Author's Name:`. Type your name and press Enter. Then WordPerfect asks you whether you want to make a letter, memo, or itinerary. Follow the prompts, and soon you'll have the basics of your letter, memo, or itinerary written out; all you need to do is type the body of the thing.

Reselect a Block (Alt-B)

When you block text and turn on some feature like Bold, WordPerfect takes the highlight off the block. Sometimes, though, you'll want to do more than one thing to that block. For example, you might want to make it bold *and* italic. Well, after you've turned on one feature for the blocked text, press Alt-B to reblock the text so that you can turn on another feature.

Insert a Blank Line (Alt-I)

Every once in a while, you might want to put a blank line above the current line. Just move the cursor anywhere in the line you want to be below the blank line. Then press Alt-I.

Replace One Attribute with Another (Alt-R)

This shortcut is magnificent when you want to change all your under-lined text to italic text or trade some other text emphasizers. Move the cursor to where you want to begin replacing an attribute. Press Alt-R and follow the prompts. This shortcut works much like the regular Replace feature except that it can switch attributes—something the ordinary Replace can't do.

Bring Up a Calculator (Ctrl-C)

WordPerfect has a calculator you can use to perform simple addition, subtraction, division, and multiplication. Press Ctrl-C to bring up the calculator, and use your numeric keypad to do your math. Press F7 when you're done.

Place a Bookmark in your Document (Alt-M)

You're working in one part of a document when you remember some-thing you need to change earlier in the text. You'll want to be able to come back to this point without hunting. Just press Alt-M and WordPerfect puts <<MARK>> into your text at the cursor location. The next tip shows you how to get back in a jiffy.

Return to Your Bookmark Quickly (Alt-F)

If you've put a <<MARK>> in your document with Alt-M, press Alt-F to return to that spot (and get rid of the <<MARK>>) in nothing flat. This is great for returning to a spot where you were working in a document.

Extra Secret-Bonus Tip: Shortcut Cheat Sheet

It won't be easy to remember all these shortcuts, so photocopy this page, and then cut out the box below and tape it on your monitor until you're comfortable with the shortcuts you use.

Return to the main editing screen	Alt-E
Flip two characters	Alt-T
Delete an entire line	Alt-D
Send the printer a "Go"	Alt-G
Capitalize the first letter of the current word	Alt-C
Start a letter, memo, or itinerary	Ctrl-D
Reselect a block	Alt-B
Insert a blank line	Alt-I
Replace one attribute with another	Alt-R
Bring up a calculator	Ctrl-C
Place a bookmark in your document	Alt-M
Return to the bookmark	Alt-F

I HATE

Index

G-I

grammar, checking, 99
graphics, 224
    clip art, 225
    documents, 226-229
        borders, 229-232
    lines
        deleting, 221
        horizontal, 217-218
        vertical, 218-220

hanging indents, 122
hard drives, files, deleting, 204
hard page breaks, 20
hard page returns, 172-174
headers, 144, 156-157, 176
    memos, 269
headlines, newsletters, 236
Help feature, 315
high-resolution graphics, 228
highlighting, *see* blocking
horizontal lines, 217-218
    deleting, 221
hyphenating words, 313, 318

indenting
    paragraphs, 121-122, 174
    text, 60-61, 300, 317
        hanging indents, 122
        tabs, 148-151

Initial Codes, margin and line
    settings, 312
inserting lines in text, 321
installing printers, 192
italic text, 63-64, 90, 127-129,
    174, 316
italic macro, 260-261

J-K

justification
    defaults, 165-166
    text, 175

keyboard combinations, *see* short-
    cut keys
keyboards, layout, shortcuts,
    319-323
keys
    arrow, blocking text, 82-84
    Backspace, 317
    Caps Lock, 18
    Delete, 317
    Enter, 18
    Num Lock, 318
    Tab, 18
    see also function keys; shortcut
      keys

N

O-P